MICHAEL HELLER has published more than twenty-five volumes of poetry, essays, and memoir. His recent works include the poetry collection *This Constellation Is a Name: Collected Poems 1965–2010*, *Dianoia*, and *Beckmann Variations and Other Poems*, a work in prose and poetry. He is the recipient of numerous prizes, including awards from the Poetry Society of America, the National Endowment for the Humanities, and the Fund for Poetry. He lives in New York City.

Michael Heller

Telescope
Selected Poems

NYRB/POETS

 NEW YORK REVIEW BOOKS *New York*

THIS IS A NEW YORK REVIEW BOOK
PUBLISHED BY THE NEW YORK REVIEW OF BOOKS
435 Hudson Street, New York, NY 10014
www.nyrb.com

Library of Congress Cataloging-in-Publication Data
Names: Heller, Michael, 1937– author.
Title: Telescope : selected poems / by Michael Heller.
Description: New York : New York Review Books, 2019. | Series: New York
  Review Books Classics |
Identifiers: LCCN 2019017899 (print) | LCCN 2019018919 (ebook) | ISBN
  9781681374079 (epub) | ISBN 9781681374062 (paperback)
Subjects: | BISAC: POETRY / American / General.
Classification: LCC PS3558.E4762 (ebook) | LCC PS3558.E4762 A6 2019
  (print) |
  DDC 811/.54—dc23
LC record available at https://lccn.loc.gov/2019017899

ISBN 978-1-68137-406-2
Available as an electronic book; ISBN 978-1-68137-407-9

Cover and book design by Emily Singer

Printed in the United States of America on acid-free paper.
10 9 8 7 6 5 4 3 2 1

Contents

NEW POEMS

FROM

A Look at the Door with the Hinges Off (2006)

Poems from the mid-1960s

7 Praises

Be drunk.
Be the body
drunk. Drunk.

Move to become;
be
ruffled.

Wind become.
Be as
brought here.

Be loosed.
Be kept.
Be loosed. Lost.

Wind you are;
know it.
Be light.

Find light.
Be found
as in it.

Be,
as being is.
Be born.

OK Everybody, Let's Do the Mondrian Stomp

small red block
beside a long
white block

tall white
block beside
a large

white block
yellow block
under the

tall white block
then a small
white block

and a long
white block
and a

blue block
locked
in a corner

One on the Muse

Once, there were eyes, then ears...

The age existed, exists; it streams continually
out of a disfigured mouth

And where you are going or have been,
the words erode

the continuity you call
yourself

Now, how differently
you will wear your pants

and stand multiplied in the garden in a
new sun's light—

After you've examined the flowers
will all of you then

go home

Fragment

the hidden harmony is better —Heraclitus

laughed

         thought of the coins
         beside

the wrinkled Kleenex

                is the shoe?
how "this age"
     will bear it   to be
                  excluded   the hand
against
your knowledge: her
secrets, what

she looked like   your eye

says everyone at once

excludes design of
spontaneity   and that

before us stretch

the young girls'

         neither firm
         nor soft

perfection

A Look at the Door with the Hinges Off

1

In white suits, on a whitewashed terrace, Pound and Fenollosa sat at a white-painted wrought-iron table with a glass top, drinking a milky white drink, ouzo perhaps or a mixture of milk and water. At that time, Fenollosa had grown a rather large black mustache which stood out against the whiteness of the scene like one of his inimitable Chinese characters.

2

In white suits, pagination permitted, the terrace washed in white paint, a light rain had fallen, which now the heat of the sun, pulsating behind the clouds, changed to steam. Ouzo was brought out by the waitress, a young girl with very white skin whose dark eyes hung in the white space of the scene like two dots in the negative of a photograph taken through a telescope trained on Sirius and Canis.

3

In control of the whites, Franz Kline claimed he was not a calligrapher, painting the white portions of his later canvases with as much concern as he showed for the blacks. Canis and Fenollosa would have gotten along well together.

4

We have a problem with white. It is the grace of saying it. Something we like—a flash of color, an absolute aimlessness to our intensity—the world will suffer less.

5

At every point a node of energy clung to the white wool of her dress. It was all very sexy.

6

The grand themes demand a certain silence, a sense of quietude which precludes pompous utterance. Here, my dearest, the ubiquity of the world in clean white sheets.

FROM

Earth and Cave (2006)

Poems from 1966

White plumed reeds
above yerba buena
—a clear dry smell

but the fact of nature
so complexly given

I was no more of it
than you, a swift
mindless carrier beyond,
beyond that one
so perfectly real
in wanting, and
no thought then
seemed deeper

White plumed
sea reeds
a tassel

a keepsake
of no wisdom

Buriana Beach

the tall weeds
weathered white
a screen behind the horse
nuzzling at grass fringe
on which the field hand put son
and the horse stepped
dignified up and down the beach

past the German girl in bikini
whose sex   later
bare backed   he must have felt
—astride him
her beauty was unmistakable
and when the horse reared,
the very image of mounting,
as she on him—
forelegs and cock
flailing air—
this
            she held to

                    ◆

sun up
the keels of the boats up
the men sleep under
eyes and cockpits
of those open boats
turned from sky—a blue
one cannot know
and not return to

—so easily tossed
in sea

"I was told hardly any
learn to swim, they go out too far...night
...anguish...
to try
to make it back"

the old men
the survivors
they come to live in daylight
mending nets

or older
sitting quietly on the *Paseo*
shielding their eyes
from the sun   or what?

Dream

And the rain clouds ripped loose from the deeply colored peaks of the Sierra Morenos. *All you wanted then.* As if your nature were a parched lip and the soft tendrils of cloud your oasis. For under all this, under this sky of turbulence and unfulfilled promise, the countryside lay which in honesty you did not belong to. And the rain was a symbol, in that both of you desired to receive it.

This fact pierced me with sudden aloneness. I had no words, even for my wife. That is, I remember leaving the house day after day. To walk in the fields. *You walked in the fields.* You were a curiosity. To the field hands, to the beetles with their bright enameled backs. Stopping to let the attentions wander. An absurd elusive sense of self, all the more alive because what seemed to slip away was just that attention, the holding of which was proof, at least in words, of the term "alive."

The beetles: since everything was of equal importance. I mean none of it was unimportant. The grass alive with them crawling obliviously over my shoe. The pure perfect life of the beetle, which sickened me. The beetle which might drown in the symbolical rain. If it rained. For the dream could not undercut the geography.

FROM

Accidental Center (1972)

In the difficulties of the rough seas
of the passage—for that
is what it was—a thing to be endured,
but for the beauty of the powerful lunges
of the dolphins seen
from the deck, a wildness
in the seas, as wild as seas
and natural, as we knew
ourselves not
in the blindered shuttered salon
as the heart jumped
when the rose
and its fluted vase
fell to the table
after an untoward roll

                      —untoward as the steel meaning
unbending of the ship's prow
or the rock's entrapment
against which, a wild sea
and wild dolphins...
                   kinship
and miscalculation

Pressure:

Didn't you say you loved me?

under what conditions

under what
under what
under what

_____

under the air
@ 15 lbs per square inch on the roof
on the safety-factored I-beams
                        slipping down thru curtain walls
to the ground
to gravitational bedrock
                    accidental center: home

                    ◆

which we sailed from

under black
and glitter

irony
and smugness
facing out on the frozen rocks
of the universe

the hard energy

spectral pinpricks

excitations given and received

the pulsar's wave peak
falling from enormous source
on the steel mesh of the antenna
drowning the signal of the probe
impaled on the far-off planet

whim and fantasy and power

◆

the radio at sea
the monstrous groans of the empty airwaves
for two days
midpoint Atlantic

now
to face ourselves
amid the gush of plumbing
the whir of ventilators packing air into the cabin

◆

My God
            what we felt
one night on the deck
of the *Novi*
                        the beat of engines
thru her plates
                                    overhead

the tenuous milk clouds

their silent movements

myriad possibilities

concrete and eternal

spaced as waves

feel THIS
                she said, wanting desperately my participation

awash in the bombarding cosmic rays
in the mysterious cosmos
itself on the heights
of cause and being

Three Bar Reflections on John Coltrane

The language of New York has changed a bar and
                                    restaurant
scene to two women talking of lovers black and white,
liberal lovers. She says she saw a man on the street
roughly of his features and mistook the man for him but
that the man was not his color. She says to her friend,
she is color blind, she says she knows all about him.

◆

He: a hunched back and boiling red face; beside she: small
and shriveled. Both in the booth, their ugliness uglier
for their awareness. This couple getting thru the world.
A fact imaging a deeper fact. As with only the weight
of notes the song is dragged down thereby amid detritus
and effluvia. Against the sweetness of creation attitudes
are posed because *it* drives back to the core thru all
the secret lives dreamt of, rancorous and jealous of
what is incomplete or unfulfilled overwhelming the music
unless love saves it.

◆

History is a joke. Personal history: unfunny.
Knowing everyone to be serious when sick and banging
on the bed for some stranger, but that he should be
like ourselves. And come get drunk or delirious, falling
into someone resembles us. On this, the heart realizes
itself meaningless—its words have moved off beyond

their meanings, as in the music, the whorls of sound are an eternal trope—an eternal equivalency. Not to be admitted to my world—I come to his.

Paragraphs

I

The duck drapes its head gracefully over
its back. Then, after an instant in which
its neck forms a supremely natural arch,
slips its head silently under water,
after which a percentage of the body
follows. Ponge, who wrote of *L'Huître*
and *un coquillage*, is pleasantly evoked
by the re-emergence of that part of
the duck formerly submerged followed by
the duck's bill in which there is a water snail
After some time the duck which has waddled
onto the grass, or at least that part of
the duck once wet, is again dry.

II

One does not come into being in the
manner of a rock. That that manner is still
a mystery does not disfigure
the discrepancy. The rock, if it at
some other time, was not this rock,
had, at that other time, an equally
enviable condition. That is, for itself
it has no history. I imagine the repair
or heal of all that is, i.e., Creation,
to be the attainment of just such a similar
state. Thus, to be occupied solely with one's

own sense of presence which means to live
without consequence.

III

Finding sense to change. Making
form as from the last form. Being
beast after amoeba. A panoply of
shapes hints at the processional.
If things come, then go—as the
Sage relates—a sense of passage stays
the purely inevitable. Certainly the
mind in its final shape will efface
history by finding an ability to
neatly end itself.

IV

Looked at from a scientific view-
point: do not imagine, do not
represent for yourself, but acquire
the qualities of a giant red star.
Cooling in intergalactic space, the
great web coalesces—its mode asymp-
totically parallels the end of
Duration and the beginning of a
glorious Entropy in which conflict
is not eliminated but is no longer
contextual (a steady state). Space,
that other product of the angels, will thus
continue to exist. That is, with the
universe, all you are (or all they

are) will go out. Grace, then, or the
notion of such *sans terminus*.

V

In every great rumination, one discovers
the same death. The poets grow in a
brittle age, most talkative when at
heart most silent. They know how each
word is a shift of matter, yet how
beyond them, of itself, matter
moves, and how that energy is Joyous
or Tragic but always Comic. This, then,
prepares the future corridors of the
years, a time softened for our coming:
the air, chromium at the windows, our
bodies experiencing the imprint of
stars.

Knowledge (1979)

Knowledge

To think a man might dream against this
This something simpler than metaphor

The world
Which spoke back
In facts, to him

That heavy pageantry

Yet when the life or when the bed
Was empty
He'd lay his head
Among the voices of the dead

It was his child and his childhood
It was coats and books
Heaped in a room
Toys and an ache

Bialystok Stanzas

from a book of old pictures

I

Light—
The scene filled with photographer's light

This sparsely furnished room
In the corner of which
A china-closet Ark

The old men
Under green shaded bulbs
Reading Torah

The prayers are simple,
To what they think larger
Than themselves
—the place almost bare,
Utterly plain

The flat white light
Adds no increment
But attention

2

He sits in the armchair
Beside his bed

In his hands
A Yiddish paper

On his head
A high black
Pointed yarmulke

The room's things
Furnished by donation
Reads a small brass plaque
Above the headboard of the bed

A bed, a hat upon his head

A *yizkor* glass, the candle for the dead
Burnt down, the wax scraped out

He uses it for drinking

3

Shiny linoleum
You can almost
Smell the pine oil

The beds
A few feet apart

So the old men
Tired of the world
In the evening
Can face each other
And talk

But now the shades are half pulled up
Sun streams in the windows

The room almost empty
But for the two directors
Sitting stiffly on chairs
Who, like the white painted beds,
Seem supremely
Official

At one side
Two gray bedridden men
Finished too with dignity
Are giggling

4

The old bind with phylacteries
—between the leather turns
The pinched flesh bulges, the old
Skin, the hairs burn

As if to do this is also
For the pain
—to explain
To Him of what it is
They are made

Thus, why they fail

5

This one and that one
Look like madmen
With their long wisps of hair
They scream: I chant, I dance
Like a crab

In the room the women wail
A plangent erotic note
Their loins itch with double fire
As he in topcoat-who-is-blessed
Bestirs them
Screams their demons back

Until their innocence
Stands naked as desire

Oy, Oy
He whirls, he spins
Till the beard is out
From his face like a flag

And in wild wisdom
Throws her to the boards

She, who would
That next instant
Have pulled him down to her
But for the trick
Of the ritual

6

THE JEWISH FIRE COMPANY

There was one fireman none knew
Neither his family nor friends
He had good eyes, though they looked
A little wild. He was sent
To the watchtower

One day, almost at once,
Two fires broke out in town
The Hasid grocer's
And a gentile butcher

The fireman warned
Of the butcher's blaze
But said nothing about the grocer
Whose place burned to the ground

When what he had failed to do
Was discovered and explanation demanded
He said: Those who do not
Follow our God's way
Must be helped
And those who do
Must accept his justice

— — — — — — — — — — — — — — —

This one joined
So the young ladies
Should see him in uniform

They did
And flattered the brass and the leather
But not him

Finally, he charmed a farm girl
Of pious family into the fields
And in the manner of the orthodox
Threw his cap to the hay
Where he thought to take her

To his delight, she bent toward
The straw, raising her skirt
As she kneeled. Suddenly,
She whisked the cap up
Tucked it in her girdle and ran away

So ashamed was he
The next day he left for Warsaw

Years later, the farm girl
Place the cap on her firstborn's head

7

TERRIBLE PICTURES

Page 147

Snow—
A group of people
Awkwardly caught

They have just discovered
The photographer, and he, them

The old man with the sack
Who has turned
Shrugs his disbelief into the lens

No sense of emergency
In the pose
Could be as real

Page 153

Grimly
They lie closely packed
Upon each other
In the mass grave

Looking now
Like figures of saints
Carved across cathedral doors

—but beyond image or irony,
The empty wrongness.

Here, all death
Was made untimely

Page 163, Caption:

"fought in the streets to the very end
and perished by his own hand
with the last remaining bullet"

Page 164, Caption:

"died in the ghetto"

Page 166, Caption:

"fell in battle ... 1944"

Page 168, Caption:

"killed ..."

Page 157, Burnt Synagogue

This light—
A river through which
Another life poured

Figure and ground
Of how the dark
Informs the light

Brings forth bodies, faces
Brings forth
The things of the earth
That we see to completion
—beloved, hated—

But that life was broken forever
Here, look, look, this is but
Its mirror

Only the mirror remains

And gone—
Whole peoples are gone
To horror beyond remonstrance—

Freitogdige
Donershtogdige
Shabbosdige
Consumed in those fires

Words can add nothing
That flame itself was without a light

*The Yiddish names above were those given by the
citizens of Bialystok to the victims of three mass
executions: "the Friday dead," "the Thursday dead,"
"the Saturday dead."*

8

FROM THE ZOHAR

The blue light
            having devoured
All beneath it:
            the priests,
The Levites, etc....
                  Now the prayerful ones
Gather
            at the flame's base
Singing and meditating
            while above the lamp glows,
The lights, in unity, are merged
Illumined world
            in which above and below
Are blessed

9 (CODA)

SENILE JEW

One God. One boiled egg.
Thirty *dy-yanus*, and the Paradise
Not yet given a number.

Eight nights, eight lights
Which break the dark
Like a cat's wink.

I think the boot is not gone—
Whose boot? I ask
Do you wear the boot?
Or does he who wears the boot
Wear you?

Coat of my pain, cloth
Of pain, winding sheet of
My horror. Just a rag,
Just a *shmata*. You
Are not my pain, not you.
My pain is me: I am the Jew.

After Montale

Nothing which seems particularly large.
The poet catches the mere termite
Busy at its burrowing. Then that fellow
Disappears, and only the hole
Is left.

All this took was time.
And we wonder what it is
That time itself creates or excretes
Or simply disappears into. What hole
It leaves.

In the Park

On the bench,
Sitting in the woman's lap, a grown man

A pietà seen
At ten removes of time and place

Making the story's end
Suddenly its beginning

Mother, I remember
That red peaked broken union
Which was your breast

And know no older wound
Of memory

Invited and lost,
Invited and fled

And my life again a broken tale
—not for truth, but *to please you*—
Which I have to tell

At Albert's Landing

with my son

I

The path winds. You are around a bend
Unseen. But your voice
Crackles in the walkie-talkie
You made me bring. "Here's a leaf,
A tree." The detail,
Not the design, excites you.
I don't know what to say.
After months in the city,
I'm feeling strange in the woods.

II

Spongy ground.
Matted leaves
Beneath which lie
Dirt, bones, shells.
Late April: milky light
And warmth. Thinnest odors rise.
In the middle of one's life
More things connect
With dying, what's come,
What's over.

III

It is said
That what exists is like the sky

Through which clouds pass. I suspect
That mine is a poetry of clouds.
Above me, some wispy tuft catches sun
In an interesting way. *The naked very thing.*
I'm glad of this, don't look
In the billowy mass
For the teased-out shape
Of a horse's head or a bird's wing.
Yet finding it now and then,
Unsummoned: some thought or image,
Recalling how each
Depends on each.

IV

Together we follow the trail's twists
Until the pond.
There, two white egrets
Stand against the high brown grass.
Intent watching
Is almost timeless, but some noise
One of us makes scares them off.
They rise over our heads, circle
Out of sight. Strange sadness
Grips me. The after-image
Of their shapes still burns.

V

Here we are in some fugal world.
Tree branches make a kind of tent.
And the squirrel, when he eats,

Looks like a little man. And here
You fling your arms out
Whirling around at the frightened
Skimming ducks. The duck's eye,
Like ours, must be its center. We
Are alone, rooted in our aloneness.
And yet things lean and lean,
Explaining each other and not themselves.
I call you; it's time to go.

VI

Different as the woods are
This is no paradise to enter or to leave.
Just the real, and a wild nesting
Of hope in the real
Which does not know of hope.
Things lean and lean, and sometimes
Words find common centers in us
Resonating and filling speech.
Let me know a little of you.

Postulates

Loss is more complex than gain
Though neither completely understood.
One remembers
He was five, six, seven years old.
To the fact of the memory
The memory stands
As an axe to wood. Wood, ourselves,
In the streamings and contours,
The roughened grain.

Make a mark on me.

Speculum Mortis

Angled toward you in the glass,
Mind wanting ease
I think, Mother, we scarcely look alike.

And yet, the "doctor of grief"
May do no more than be a little slothful.

And the light is
As from a nonreflective dark

And invades the mirror's space.
A hollow strangely lit,

A light, sourceless,
Radiant

As any truth,
Disfiguring all one thinks one is.

Interminglings

to J.A.

I

Sun on the begrimed windows,
Light and dust curiously arrayed.

Infused with each other, falling
On the bed, on ourselves where we lie.

Finite life in the pattern's
Verge and shift, in the hovering dust.

In the beam's slant,
Designs almost infinite.

I know, in my heart,
This nature is all aesthetic.
Each, resolved, being something like a story.

Story of ourselves
In these curves and tangles,

In the half-light.
What I wanted to say

Was that in truth, we each
Could have picked, could have
Found ourselves

Among any of these.

II

Many years given
In belief of the body's sadness

A thickness, as of the throat
In the world.

From there, the voice telling
Into its knotted web
Of glints and darknesses.

Perhaps you are moved as I am,
Lifted in some strange way
By the plunge into sorrows.

Facing each other, these recognitions:
Two small animals, quiverers,

Aware they can be hurt.
And sometimes, nothing,

Not even the severe lines
Of your body, which wildly delight

Bring me this close to you.
For all that is different,

How each in our life
Is alike.

III

We agreed. No one's quite written out
A philosophy of affluence, least of all
This affluence I'm feeling today.

What strikes in the world,
A curious kind of comfort

Where bug and leaf, or better, bug
And garbage in the street, are joined.

The broken hydrant almost sings a warble.
The undersides of clouds, sulphurous green and red.

Crossing the Bowery to your place,
"marks of weakness, marks of woe."

Strange, ugliness and loveliness
Both slash the heart.

No shelter: we are exposed
Like the weed shooting through the rubble,

Like the tree's small roots
Which curl at the stone, at the broken pipework.

Almost part of, and not against.

To imagine this
Is what is workable.

That the spring did not come

To enrage the tree...

And I think now of the open bow of your back,
Tremor which ends, which does not end.

The gesture sears.
The cursive graves its line in me.

This remains the one gift.
This alone is unconfused.

IV

ABOVE WESTCLIFFE

All this living, dying.
The town lights seem barely pinched
Out of the folds of darkness

And the moon, so lovely, so far,
Full-blown tonight into a dream's indifference
Riding solitary above the black pines

The skunk waddles and the deer
Comes to lick at the salt block
Ghastly in the whiteness, perversely
Monumental—

They move with the rest
Through the eye's frame of
This beautiful pointlessness

I too arrive without exactly having
Taken myself—my *self*, whatever
In this moment, that is.

Where, that depth?

And the chart and the star book
Are strange counsel. The fixities themselves
Are caught in their slow turn
And go under the world
Like human time, like human death.

The candle sputters, dies in the room
Burning all, chair, bed, bodies into shadow
—breast, thigh, you, me
And the light and dark pour their grainy liquid
Into that wave that bears up love, succor, pity
In a transmigratory arc.

Stanzas on Mount Elbert

Where we climbed in the berserk air
Of trails, sharp spikey views
And dizzying vertigo. I watched
Marmot and pika dart
Among lichen-covered rocks
Envying not their agility
But that they survive
On such apparent bleakness.

Then, seeing you on the path above,
Aspen crook in hand, orange poncho
Bannered to the wind, the painter's
Famous *Wanderer in the Clouds*,
Whatever passes between us,
Whoever you are, in that moment
You were a guide to me. We took
The path six inches at a time: with each
Breath a step; with each step a breath,
Sounds of ourselves reverberating
In hollows, in great brown cratered cups of rock
Until what was human seemed to be passing
Into its sheer facticity.

And by the summit, head abuzz in thin air,
Pain or joy or confusion heaped as one
Into the round bulge
Of the mountain's endlessness, it was
Almost too comical to have walked there,
To worship at that feast of obstacles.

And the lakes four thousand feet below
Leered crazily. I think
We were looking back
At what does or does not exist,
What the mind mirrors; something
To which we do not so much return
As turn to, though the turning hurts.

Mourning by the Sea

"sough incessant"

Your father died, mine dies.
Mothers, sisters, brothers still.
Dark harbor water mottled green and blue.

Before us on the sand,
The crab claw severed,
The bivalve crushed, the shell in shards.

The *on* then *off* of this is hard.
The place,
The boundary edge—

Where picked from off its ledge
The polyp dissolves
At the gull's stomach wall.

This is not spring; this is not fall.
The brush tips all.
Your eyes, your laugh—

To see one living is to see by half.
The body changes before the eyes:
Dust dark in light the sun burns.

Such light on waves is curve and turn,
End seeding end.
And the image then that wants to come,

Thin as air,
Is nothing but words: terror and fear,
No self and no recurrence.

In the Builded Place (1989)

*Circles and right lines limit and close
all bodies, and the mortall rightlined
circle (Θ The Character of Death) must
conclude and shut up all.*

—Sir Thomas Browne, *Urn Burial*

With a Telescope in the Sangre de Cristos

There
Where the mountains bulked
Above the valley floor

And town and ranch lights
Made shallow bowls
Into other heavens

Raw nature actually seemed less raw.

Again and again that night
The glass checked
In its round frame

The nebula's thumbprint swirls:
This fine life of bonds and connections...

Then
I looked in
At another's eyes

Looked past that image
Of the self,
In at the pupil's black hole

Where light gives up
The granular,
Becomes a maelstrom

Grinding
Beyond the phenomenal
To a lightless, frightening depth.

O this fine life of bonds and connections...

Father Parmenides

Neither great nor small
The hollow simply is.

Like the wine of its cask, the voice
Empties the speaker, empties
Even the void at fullness.

Moon Study

To steal a look at it as the tide pulls,
And the earth, sheathed in the living
And the nonliving, bulges and dimples

At the surface of the seas. The moon!
It appears beyond my capacity
To do more than give it name, to shout

Like the haiku master, O bright!
O bright! O moon! as though
With a word I could embrace

some lucent teaching of its being. To have
No hold on this architect of shadows, this
Realm of space, of airless peaks, fantastical...

America, tranquil and monumental under
the hard moon, is also a dream of cold light
Raining purity of cities alabaster.

And now, sister of the obdurate,
How the body of love gleams otherworldly,
Exotic with distance and intimacy. O pallid!

O nightmares of wars and terrors, O terrible
Bright! The great pocked surfaces,
Craters of the moon, craters of the bomb,

These two texts have swallowed *cri de coeur*,
Ode and epistle, our books of loss.
In the restless night, at the window,
My white ego meets that white eye.

In the Builded Place

I wander thro' each charter'd street —Blake

In the unfair life
Of this night or any other,
In this city,

Someone's broken world,
In the streetlamp's
Small circle of light,

To find no magic aura, no blaze
Of clarity on the broken littered pavement,
To find neither justice

Nor penance of lives, to find
Only the absurd arrangements and disarrangements:
A slum block in the light's cool bath of truth.

◆

Who will it hurt that tonight
This broken world is but a literal?
Who will it hurt to note

The light on a woman's face?
To see her face pend in time?
Can it hurt to note

The weight of time
Weighing down the lovely features,
Unable to break loose

From that which it weighs upon.
It suggests no more than you resolve this:
The gross weight of life in time

Looking to be resolved in meaning,
Solved in love.

◆

Tonight the clatter of failed myths,
Of hierarchies, dies. Tonight
We are joined as one in the streetlamp's light,

A corrosive light: dissolve, dissolve,
Discovering selves in the core of world,
That lonely need. So that we may arrive at last

In late dusk, in late time,
Bare islands of the human archipelago...
I stand back, watch the light on the curves

Of her face, not so much to feel
That rush of movement in me,
As to see again the quick and the alive

Open under open air.

◆

And the sky's curve
Lies against the curve of the city.
Streets, people caught in thickness

Of event. And the eye and mind are led
To the moon's loft, to the bird aquiver,
To the serpent's gentle coil.

That they connect,
Connect like consciousness
In concentric whorls

Or like stations of the cross
Through loves, hates, errors...
These flimsy beatitudes of order.

Well-Dressing Rounds*

Ashford in the Water, Derbyshire

Terrorists leave notes
on dead bodies, warnings to others
not to touch, and I remember that Antigone,
against Creon's published male tyranny,
sought to set her brother's body at rights
not with other men but with the earth.
Possibly, the city man, out in England's
green fields, puts his hand to the grass
as though touching a pliant woman,
as though renewing a pact.

Here, in Ashford, flowers blaze,
bedeck the fields and woods.
And again, my hand sweeps as though
to gather this world to the fable book
where it once lived. But I'm a tourist,
with my own stories, walking
to the wellheads and to the bridge.

Last week, a printed handout reads,
schoolchildren gathered plants
and flowers among the trees,
pulled petals from blossoms,
plucked seeds from pod and husk,
gathered tufts of fur from rabbit pelts.
The teachers must have shown them how.
I read, and I'm with tourists, whose nations
divide up seas and lands while we walk
to wellheads and to the bridge.

Hands of children shaped
the crude, broad Marys and the Christs
with outstretched arms made of flower
upon part of flower, corn and pea
lining borders, all pressed
into now dried plaster. They ready
this bloodied world as though it were
a benison, *rise up o earth*—
the message as we talk and walk
round the basins of the wells.

Flowers are everywhere in Ashford.
It is midsummer; children dance the maypole
for visitors who come to walk the circuit
of the wells. Water rises up; it sparkles
in the sun, water of which we're made,
of which we drink, and this is what they honor
as we walk from the wellheads to the bridge.

*In certain towns in Derbyshire, the ancient wells are dressed
(decorated) each year during the period of the midsummer
solstice.

Mythos of Logos

First the stars or the patterning of stars in darkness, and then perhaps someone climbing up a mountain to close the gap. Begins in dusty foothills, then forest, then high empty tundra and piles of rock, and at the top to brush at with the hand the spangled emptiness. But the hand feels nothing, sweeps nothing but the cold air. The loveliness of blackness for the first time brings solitude. And then one keeps silence at failure, nurses anger and shame, swallows the bitter taste.

And so the world becomes another place, and now I must confess to the many things that I forgot to say, was afraid to say, for fear, for love, for shame, O ancients and splendid hosts whose words come before and after,

Who have uttered out, one theory goes, what was written in the gene codes and in the stars' imprints before our speech. And now, those lucid structures are gantries to my nights, wheeling and reassembling.

And yes, the whole career is night, is crafted out of silence. And so the sentences out there were not unsaid, nor did they blow away with stellar dust and stellar time. They settled down about my head, resembling a dome the exact shape of my skull hidden from others by a flap of skin.

After Plato

To the poet: not to be original.
No heart can fully voice itself.
No public so bemused to follow.

How to bear a poem whose truth
Would sear the sky, a bright sun
Rising per schedule. More heat,

More sweat, more guilt to add
To toil? Poet, spend your days
Surmising cloud banks of which

There are a vast sufficiency.
Praise occluded forms:
Your blinded loves, your hates.

Too dull? Too milky in their lucence?
Think of horrors when in the calm
Someone thought they saw the light.

Squint and wait for shifts of wind
To put shapes on chance maneuvers.
Ah, ruins afloat! See, your little

Nostalgia requires no contrastive blaze.
With luck, clouds will break
To rend familiars. This, the more-
Than-moment of the blinded reader.

As though, for you, a god
Had meant us sightless. As though
An eyelid had been peeled back
Only to insert a cinder.

Homer Timeless

His way was not his way, but being blind
His way was that much more attuned to death.

Some called him camp follower; others claimed
He justified Achilles' gloom, the tide of which
Had thrown down cities.

At the pyre, Achilles had Troy's twelve highborn
Slain. "This," the poet said, "was an evil thing."

Yet he also showed the bright blade's
Flashing beauty. He was accused:

He did not report the real war. The listener
Listens, remembers what he will remember.

◆

It is said the wave break off Hellas metronomes
His lines. What more noble than this mime of giving,

More honorable than to stay with his words
While outside, beyond the chair, is flesh and rubble.

Take the gift of his rhythms.

And after one is emptied by war, knots
Of one's stomach nodules of ice, to imagine

Oneself among the maimed and rotting, the beach
Where once the sea was red with burning ships.

They could not go home. And while he spoke,
The Greece he spoke of made new Iliums

As newfound lands make new births.

Photograph of a Man Holding His Penis

for Michael Martone

World o world of the photograph, granular,
Quantumed for composition in the film's grain,
But here blurred, soft-toned and diffuse
Until the whole resolves into an ache, a
Chimerical, alchemical flower, a pattern
Against pure randomness.

As though the process itself exists to mock
What is discrete, is singular. Dot leans on dot,
On the binary of *only two* can make of one a life.

And the myth is partial,
A dream half of need confused with desire.

I too live out this fear, this shadowed aloneness,
The white hand's delicate hold where the genital hairs
Are curled, the groin become a hermitage, a ghastly
Down of our featherings . . .

And the texture is bitter, bifurcate,
A braille of flesh
From which a ghost is sown.

Today, Somewhat After Dante

The wind is blowing; the wind bends everything
but the human will. Thus war and pillage
have written more on the earth's surface than wind.

The Wars, Vietnam, the Greater and Lesser Holocausts,
these names, like those of the Florentine treacheries,
season whatever paradisiacal truth to poems.

Yet, today, I fall like a blunt object into respites,
walk forgetful among the windblown shrubs
and brackish estuaries on this day of unplanned sun,

happy to be lost in the world's things,
in all this matter and *dura mater*, to feel
when I speak, in each word, a sweet tensile pull of a string.

Afternoon light is penetrant, a blank, absented
fixity. What birds have flown off I will find
in glossaries; old loves I will find in

the mind's book between a cloud and a branch or
a filament of moon in the intense blue. And perhaps
I will stumble, as in a vision, on all the dead,

mother and father included, lining the shore
of Little Tick Island where they will be busy bowing
to that figure of perfect freedom, their selfsame minds.

And in the distance, like a memory
of love's midpoint, I'll see the sun flash white
on the salt-caked weather sides of twisted trees.

Heteroglossia on Fifty-Third

Streets of a city, I walk and lose the hour.
Today, unsure of what I write, I circumambulate
the new and the ruin, find it
twelve noon amidst museums and gleaming limousines.
A bag lady shouts "I am entitled!" I also
am entitled to my thoughts at least, yet all day,
dream or nightmare do my talk, undo my walk,
so I let talk pitch self into doze or dream and chat:
man, woman, testicle, dessert. The language falls,
a chunk of disembodied sound through space.

My body sometimes feels like a corpse, but talk hears talk,
and I'm entitled in the streets, astride the century's
fatted calf, the pavement-glutted bowel. The talk of
street people is a groaning, each to each; I have heard
them singing on the trash. Ghost words, ghost fuckers!
They utter their words right out to do their ravaging
in me, joining my dead lords of speech like animals
granted province over those on whom they prey.

Montaigne

This bundle of so many disparate pieces
is being composed in this manner:
I set my hand to it only
when pressed by too unnerving an idleness,
and nowhere but at home.

I want to represent the course
of my humours; I want people
to see each part at its birth.

I have grown seven or eight years
older since I began, not
without some new acquisition.

Through the liberality of the years
I have become acquainted
with the kidney stone.

It was, precisely, of all the accidents
of old age, the one I feared most.
For my soul takes no other alarm

but that which comes
from the senses
and the body. I have at least

this profit from the stone:
that it will complete what I have
still not been able to accomplish,

to reconcile and familiarize myself
completely with death.

The more my illness oppresses me
the less will death be something
to fear.

God grant that in the end, if its sharpness
comes to surpass my powers, it may not
throw me back to the other extreme, no less
a vice, of loving and desiring death....

I have always considered that precept
formalistic which so rigorously and precisely
orders us to maintain a good countenance
in the endurance of pain.

What matter if we twist our arms,
provided we do not twist our thoughts.
Philosophy trains us for ourselves,
not for others, for being, not seeming.

It is cruelty to require of us
so composed a bearing. Let this care
be left to the actors and teachers of rhetoric.

If there is relief in complaining,
let it be so. If we feel pain evaporates
somewhat for crying out,

or that our torment is distracted,
let us shout right away. If we play
a good game, it is a small matter
that we make a bad face.

Sestina: Off-Season

These are the poets' times, these dark times,
for the world takes as real its own fanatic thought.
A realibus ad realiora, the words build a hexagram
of stagnant heavens while peasants do their work and fall,
the superior ones do their managing and seek reclusion
in their summerings beside the sun-blasted light of the sea.

The poet would rather borrow from the moon-puddled sea,
but how give up the coiled worm gnawing at the times,
burn up the page, put the word in reclusion
until only the sandy coasts are objects of a thought
and history can be thrown for a ten-count fall
—the cry of nothing—of ghost birds, cage, a hexagram

for poets who hexagram
their luxuries beside the sea,
who swoon and fall,
whose visions are multiples of love times
lovers, endless self-circles of thought
in secret fondness of their reclusion.

O poet, car roofs and glass glint under leafy reclusion
and one must give heart to vocabularies of the hexagram.
One must be at pains to see the world glitter in mere thought,
to see the cruelty in the lives of animals and in the high sea
of our leaders' rhetoric which downs the very times
and makes of these last grace notes a mechanic fall.

Compose; if necessary, compose against the fall.
For god's sake, leave this elysian reclusion!
Note how sea scud and birdlime mark the times,

how the lines flatten to this one sad hexagram
of hope, the moon's pearl puckering a violent sea
as poetry despairs of any cogent thought.

That poet who warned of unsightly sifting sands of
    thought
entered into the very end of time's articulated fall
where every word is borne upon a flood as if heaven's sea
were an earth of inundated lands. Uncover! Mind performs
    reclusion
as though recounted lives were pent beneath a hexagram
of yarrow stalks, spelling, in emboldened crumblings, our
    times.

Too long is the word disembodied from our pain while
    reclusion
buffers body. Unbuild this great vast hexagram
whose rigid lines misprision poets from loves' times.

Statue: Jardin du Luxembourg

The grass tips rise, pale white field daisies
grow in clumps, green surrounded by sandy gravel,
paths, benches, statuary, students having their lunch
in the bright sun, oo la la all this in French.

The grass reads out the Father's epoch, obscure
and bound in creation's knot, and the epoch of the Son
squats in the greensward, in curved bronze
captured in upthrust: *Les Étudiants de la Résistance.*
No comfort in the patina's uncanny cold, in the hollow
structure of the Patriarch's leg to which the youthful
    figures cling.

Our epoch is to live with these two,
Father and Son in time, to repeat endlessly
these cycles of grass and bronze. Yet Paris encircles
like our Mother, incrustations of plaster on plaster,
centuries of wear, humans stuccoed to the pile,
these little affections to outweigh a dream of monuments...

The city stretches off into sun-watered light.
To be in love with this minute is to be
in love with air displaced by metal.

On a Line from Baudelaire

at Père Lachaise

"The dead, the poor dead, have their bad hours"
If there are the dead, have they lived in vain?
Things continue, it all says, the stars bulge and quiver,
The neutrino beats, the oxidizing of metals
Heats modernity. In Paris, over the poor dead,
The tombstones fascinate, the cats hide in
Marble and shrubbery, the walls are like a vise
And enclose. Once they asked for flowers, too late,
For flowers. Green spring honors the living but who
Begged? The spring resonates with her silk; even gravel
Sings, the worm has turned me to poetry. The dead,
The powdered rich: names are taken. History spirals
Into the center of this conch shell, the air swirls
Over Paris, out of reach, lives on, dies on.
The airs of the universe beat oceanic
On these well set up stones.

Some Anthropology

And yet poems remind me of the tribe of the gentle Tasaday who some regard merely as members of another tribe taught to fool anthropologists with false primitiveness and naiveté, to be blunt in their manners and infernally innocent. No one is sure, as with poems, whether they are real or a hoax, whether the dictator, in his munificence, created a forest preserve to shelter them as he might set aside an apartment for a poet in the palace. Forests and palaces, such utopias are mostly exclusionary, like hotels for the rich, and needn't concern us. It is rainy for a rain forest to house our myths, to shelter our lost tribes, who, one by one, gather in a clearing. I sometimes think about my lost tribe of Jews, American Jews, also part hoax and part invention, whose preserve is sheltered under brick where limousines hum and one hears the faint, familiar babble of the homeless. As it happens, the Tasaday are being declared "nonexistent" by government scientists so their hardwood forests can be transformed into chests of drawers. Strange, then, the anthropology of the poet who must build his poems out of the myths he intends to falsify, who says, look my friend, you are laying away your laundered shirts in a rain forest.

The American Jewish Clock

When did Solomon (for Zalman) Heller, my grand-
father, come here, his time folded into America
like honey layered in Middle-European pastry?

When did he arrive? After his pogroms and wars,
And before my father's. Was he naive? To arrive
like an autocrat, to enter like a king, in the train

of minor victories. Zalman, here called Solomon!
With a new syllable to lengthen his name. In the vast
benumbed space of us, a little more sound to place him.

Were there sour Jewish chives on his tongue,
Yiddish chimes in the bell of his breath?
He knew very little English, but he cocked his ear.

He heard the clock sounds that translate every-
where. He had been brought into redeeming time,
each stroke the echo of his unappearing God.

With tick came the happy interregnum,
those twenties and thirties when profit
turned to loss, and loss to profit.

Tock came later when the synagogues swelled
with increase and were tethered like calves
on suburban lawns. And then...O and then,

the young walked out, walked back
to the cities, prodigals of emptied memory.
I was among them. And the door slammed shut.

And the space outside, that endlessness to America,
was ululated on every word but tick and tock.

In a Dark Time, on His Grandfather

Zalman Heller, writer and teacher, d. 1956

There's little sense of your life
Left now. In Cracow and Bialystok, no carcass
To rise, to become a golem. In the ground

The matted hair of the dead is a mockery
Of the living root. Everyone who faces
Jerusalem is turned back, turned back.

It was not a question of happiness
Nor that the Laws failed, only
That the holy or sad remains within.

This which cleft you in the possibility
Of seeing Him, an old man
Like yourself.

Your last years, wandering
Bewildered in the streets, fouling
Your pants, a name tag in your coat

By which they led you back,
Kept leading you back. My father
Never spoke of your death,

The seed of his death, as his death
To come became the seed, etc.... Grandfather,
What to say to you who cannot hear?

The just man and the righteous way
Wither in the ground. No issue,
No issue answers back this earth.

For Uncle Nat

I'm walking down 20th Street with a friend
When a man beckons to me from the doorway
Of Congregation Zichron Moshe. "May I,"
He says to my companion, "borrow this
Jewish gentleman for a moment?" I follow
The man inside, down the carpeted aisle,
Where at the front, resplendent in
Polished wood and gold, stands
The as yet unopened Ark.

Now the doors slide back, an unfolded
Promissory note, and for a moment,
I stand as one among the necessary ten.
The braided cloth, the silver mounted
On the scrolls, even the green of the palm
Fronds placed about the room, such hope
Which breaks against my unbeliever's life.

So I ask, Nat, may I borrow you, for a moment,
To make a necessary two? Last time we lunched,
Enclaved in a deli, in the dim light, I saw
A bit of my father's face in yours. Not to make
Too much of it, but I know history
Stamps and restamps the Jew; our ways
Are rife with only momentary deliverance.
May I borrow you for a moment, Nat. We'll celebrate
By twos, the world's an Ark. We'll talk in slant
American accent to code the hidden language of the Word.

Accidental Meeting with an
Israeli Poet

At the playground by the Con Ed plant,
this is strange: from tall brick stacks,
smoke is bleeding off into cloudless sky.
Little dreams, little visions must go like that.

Still, his boy and mine play in their soccer game,
each move, each kick or run precise and self-
contained. From one end of the field to the other

they go, from sun to deep shade. And there's no
poof, no gone, no fade into that all-capping blue.
Trampled ground, grass, sun-tinged webs of cable—

so this is how we reckon hope, as something
blotted up by matter that it might better
circulate in brick, in the squared-off shadows

of the power plant to commingle with children
and with games and sides, with wire and with steel
until, lo, the helmet of a soldier has sopped it up!
It sits there, insisting on a certain rightness.

And yet people's songs disperse into the air,
people's songs and rhetoric . . .

Palestine

I

Snow glides down in the West Forties.
Like a child, I could lick the snowflakes
from my wrists. In storms,
bums will nibble at the wood of tenement doorways.
The weather precipitates dreams, fantasies, I too
have my dreams of the snow's purity,
of its perfecting worlds, so little like my own.
Could I be a gentleman of this snow, my calling card
one evanescent flake to place upon a blemish?

Frankly, I'm delighted with a new scientific proof:
at any moment at least two places on the globe
must experience similar weather. Hence my
Palestine and hence my joy. Baudelaire
watched the Negress in the street stomp her feet
and imagine date palms. I don't want the territory,
just the intensity of a visit. Sh'ma Yisrael, only
the symbol world holds you and me or I and Thou.
Sh'ma Palestine, aren't you always where snow falls.

II

My Palestine, which means I love one woman,
so why not two? Which means I love that distant sky
and the lovely irritants of my inner eye. My tears

for what in life is missed. The Red Sea of my philosophy
will irrigate with salt these barren lands.

Does snow fall there too?

III

Always somewhere else, and always held by someone else...
Sweet figs, sweet thighs to Suez or Port Said.
But when snow falls one's place is yet another place.

IV

In that salty biblical sweetness, why avenge?
Grief is vectored north, east, west, the Wailing Wall.
Why avenge? Terror has cast its rigid mask,
and with fraternal semblance, transformed all
into sisters and brothers. Why avenge?
Only the dead wear human faces.

V

Yea, though I am not lifted out of sorrow,
yea, though the opus of self-regard endoweth me
for nearly nothing, I have not forgotten snow. I
have no more forgotten snow than other poets forget
time or blackbirds. I have, with love, put the snow aside,
I have let the snow melt so that I may envision Judea
as a stately gentile lady, a crusader, a crusade.

VI

I am so far away,
yet for Americans
distances are musical.
So I am near. I am with snow
which softens the city in which I live.
I am in the Forties and the snow glides down
and fills all the niches that lie between
the living and the dead.

Mamaloshon

At night, dream sentences
That will not write themselves.

And there are phrases
You forget. Dawn comes;

It's only luck
Her breast is not your mother's.

So much touched by words,
At least you live.

What escapes makes for the grave—
A respectable marker.

Constellations of Waking

*on the suicide of Walter Benjamin at the
Franco-Spanish border, 1940*

Something you wrote:
"Eternity is far more
the rustle of a dress

than an idea."
What odd sounds
to listen to

beneath occluded skies
that darken rivers,
Dnieper, Havel, Ebro,

murmuring contained
between
their treelined banks...

"In the fields
with which we are concerned,

knowledge comes only
in flashes. The text
is thunder rolling

long afterwards."
And thus, and thus...

◆

These constellations,
which are not composed of stars
but the curls of shriveled leaves

by which the tree expressed
the notion of the storm. You
lived in storm, your outer life:

"adversities on all sides
which sometimes came
as wolves." Your father—

Europe was your father
who cast you on the path,
hungry, into constellated cities:

Berlin, Moscow, Paris.
Where would
Minerva's owl alight,

on what dark branch
to display its polished
talons?

◆

1940
and in Paris, the library
is lost.

Books
no longer on the shelves—
how sweetly

they were "touched," you wrote
"by the mild boredom
of order."

◆

Curled leaf,
one among many
on trees that lead

to a border crossing.
But black wolves in France,
they have changed the idea

of eternity. Toward
Port Bou, bright dust
mixing

with the ocean's salt air.
Wavefleck from train:
each spun light

must have its meaning.
So to consider
as ultimate work

that seabed of
all citation—
you'd allow nothing of your own—

thus the perfected volume.
No author?
And then no death?

The sea is inscribed
with *The Prayer*
for the Dead. No

author and then
no death? But the leaf
acquired shadow by

the ideal of light,
scattered light
the father

never recognizes.
The books are not
on shelves,

for that was Paris.
This the closed road
from Port Bou

which glistens with the dew
of morning. Redemptive
time

which crystallizes
as tree, as leaf
on the way to a border.

Water, Heads, Hamptons

the unbearableness of idyllic literature —Canetti

My dear,
it is summer. Time to be out of time.
Let us read together the world's newspapers.

But the wind blows away the pages of the *Times*—
they rise, stretch full-length in the breeze like
any vacationer wanting a day in the sun, an even tan
to return with to a city, to proclaim "I too have been away."

Let us read. We can! Memory is our language. We are two
minds that lie athwart each other, two continental plates
with errant nationalities that articulate via subterranean grit.
In time, we will grind this world to powder, to be upraised
and bleached by processes of the seas.

But the wind blows. The surf ripples and slaps with the
    sough
of all the living and dead it has dissolved, and, with a great
respiratory suck, deposits on the beach what waves
must leave even as they take back what must be taken back.

Ah, you hear the antinoise where gusts expose the sheet
of crumpled newsprint buried in the sand. What is written
is written. But we will lean close, intent, where
windblown grains pepper the page with faint pings.

◆

It is one of those days when my will seems no more
than the will to conflate utter laziness with a poem
or with roiling sleepily in some good sex. Sleep,

O languorous sleep where I am forgetful of the misery
of history, my brutal West, a dozing prince
before which all gives way.
                              And summer
lightning at the sea's rim transforms the high
gorgeous blocks of clouds into a dance, a shadowscreen
of our imaginable gods: blue Buddha, Shiva of the knife,
Kali who follows footsteps in trackless sand, aerated
    Christ!

◆

A weird pang of nameless joy. Look, a swimmer's head
is bobbing in the sea. And I point, my finger
like a sunbeam in a barrel. Here's this head

that moves from horizon to beach, this fleshdot
that seems to swim away from the end
of an entrapping sentence, reopening its syntax,

and so, for once, is at work against
premature closure. So I identify
a brother eidolon against the tide's flat reach.

◆

Summer's paradise. Its rhythm. But not
the incessant flights of midges swarming in dark air,
alighting on the body through which hope and pain trickle,
those substantial rivers flowing to the seas.

Will you swat the tic of memory and enter into
ever-present babble of flies? Madness of words.
Old tropes like brilliance of coral shoals on which

waves break and shipwrecks and glittery cabin lights
are extinguished in the deeps.

◆

To the white sands who will speak a name?
The quiet of dusk comes back. Noiseless flight
of gulls inscribes the air and the world goes down
in a rhythm of deepening colors.

Surely the gods we invent bring out the night's phenomena:
flux into perfection, corollas and auroras, St. Elmo's fire
for all those who suffer the agonies of speech.

Objects, you
no longer offer up yourselves for ceaseless dictation,
no language anyway, our mouths are on each other.
Some lord of silence rises with stars and planets...

In the Mountains, Lines of Chinese Poetry:

the thread in the hand of a kind mother
is the coat on a wanderer's back

Before she left this world, she stitched him tight.
Today, this mountain trail's her thread, on, up and out
to endless blue, and yet there's something unrelieved
about the space, his past, his childhood is
landscaped too. His fear for her, her damaged heart.

She slept on a throne-like bed at room's end
where he and his sister were not allowed to go.
He couldn't touch her, but, from where they stood,
he'd watch her sew. She was the view, but he was in it too.

Now his thoughts of her are like the bannered clouds
that float across the alpine grass, insubstantial
before the mountain's rock, hard otherworldly fact.
He would dream her back? Was she to inhabit every fear

and every wish? Eye tug in mountain mist, he hoped,
in vacant, windblown heights, he'd find, not her, himself.
But it was only one improving stitch. She'd basted him,
    braided
thread right through his retina, her way itself defining
    sight.

Born in Water

Born in water. I was born in
my mother's water and washed out
into the world from the burst sac.

When my mother died, we respected her wishes,
collected her ashes at the crematorium,
then spread them on the grass over my father's grave.

And because the wind was blowing,
we poured water from a plastic pitcher,
and added water from our eyes
so the ashes wouldn't blow away
but seep into the ground.

Mother and father, as on the day
I was conceived, mingled together.

In Elegiacs, Birds of Florida

GULLS

Mother, those last vistas: you perched in the apartment which overlooked the wrinkled bay and the city whose patterned lights on the far shore resembled constellations. Near death, the whole world became a reading. So you too, Father. At the home, I watched with you the palm fronds wave idly outside your room. Your eyes seemed to follow shadows on the walls, mind traceries, glints and powder darks, fan waverings of now and past, sea anemone, coral branch, yielding design but inarticulate.

Short stroll between you two, about the distance gulls will leave around a solitary walker who, at sunset, skirts the water's edge. A step too close either way, and a gull will fly off, then another and another, to bob offshore on black water. Always a further horizon to inscribe a dividing line, a last blaze way out that catches the surf's turned edge. Before the salt nest of tombs, this consolation.

FLAMINGOS

Are nearly a secret. Half gawk, half grace, their thin legs hold them unsteadily erect. They teeter on nonbeing. A flock, they move as one outlandish pink-feathered thought. Something like the mind's repository of hosts and legends, their passage through the world, the double helix's cosmic joke: herd, family, tribe—how dead shades in groups are driven across the universe.

SNOWY EGRETS AND HERONS

Are ubiquitous. They fish in the inland canals behind the great hotels or at bayside, near backyards and docks of pale white homes. I have seen them hang silently in trees, eye's gift, sacs of tissue-papered fruit, the kind one buys for funerals. At sunset, they march their young across the highways and the Tamiami Trail, their nests in sleepy willows and cypress. With the beat of their wings, they have made the Everglades the other side of Lethe. They roost too beside the airport, calm and self-involved, standing at runway's end in shallow puddles amidst their own reflections.

MIND BIRDS

With my son, sitting in the park in Miami after a trip to the Parrot Jungle, we conjured up invented birds: the Guantánamo Guano-Dropping Bat, the Elixir Eider whose feathers could stuff waterbeds, the Woid Boid, the Brooklyn poet's finest fowl.

I imagine, too, the Memory Bird—O synapse that can scribe its following arc! It circles over these peopled beaches of Hades and Limbo like the fabulous Garuda, a bird which never lands nor rests. Such a creature is too expensive to feed or tame or bring to earth to lay its unblemished egg of certainty. Still, at its highest flights, its claws tear at one's heart and liver more viciously than the eagles of Prometheus.

Wordflow (1997)

Lecture with Celan

How many know
the number of creatures is endless?

So many know,
only a gasp in their questions is possible.

All that fullness—
of wounds that *won't scar over,*

pain's grille work
persisting in the memory.

What sets one free
within the sign and blesses the wordflow

without barrier?
Not literature, which is only for those

at home in the world
while air is trapped in the sealed vessel,

contained in our
containment, our relation to earth.

Omnivore language,
syntax of the real, riddling over matter,

more difficult to ken
than the Talmudic *angelus.* Thus what black

butterflies of grief
at this leaf, at this flower? Already you

have moved over ground
beyond past and future, into a strange *voiceless*ness

close to speech,
both dreadful and prophetic—all else utility

and failure. And now,
the work builds to a word's confines,

to a resemblance of lives
touching the history of a rhyme between earth and dying.

Stanzas at Maresfield Gardens

Freud's house in London, now a museum

The dream manifest as ruin. He feared forgeries
and eliminated suspicious items from the collection.

Still, after his death, many fakes were discovered.
The ruin manifest as dream. He deployed figurines

of ancient deities at which he gazed. Those with
half-turned heads he positioned over journals.

◆

His antiquities: the Buddhas, the protectors,
the instructive voids he saw in Roman jars

half-filled with a crematorium's ash and bone.
Those heaps! Their inimitable deserted air—

out of that clay and back to clay, *adamah!*
What to will from these shapeless mentors of speech?

What utterance lifting powdery blackened grains
to something human? What voice to throw out

against those other gods always in miniature in their cruel
presiding, in their fixed vesseling in bronze and stone?

Time-maimed fickle Isis-Osiris, noble Avalokitesvara
whose raised hand is a gesture to the named and unnamed

who stand guard over the scriptor. And there too,
are the onyx-faced ones, scowling at heresy and betrayal.

Do not look askance; do not miswrite! Thus, to hear
each *persona* in the room utter form, in babbled hope

of words poured back over the eons, in hope of words
given to gods as sacrifice, as exigent futures

of sound, divinities claimed in flawed obeisances.

◆

The collection was a dream unmarred by forgeries
he ruthlessly eliminated. Manifestations of half-turned heads

he thought of as ancient deployments, listening to patients
as though gazing on collections of ruined forgeries.

He deemed these manifestations as collections he deployed.
Half-turned dreams of patients gazing toward ruins,

of ancient figurines he looked at ruthlessly while journals
under deities lay open manifesting as his collections.

At the Muse's Tomb

AFTER READING

The long eerie sentences were fates as the savannahs of Georgia and the Carolinas were endless stanzas in pine and swamp water.

Searches were made among the word-habitats that mattered, consonances of landscapes and self, half-geographies contoured from remembrances, shadowed and opaque.

The rest, the unexplained, the transparency, the mirrors and the dust, were to be talked away as dreaming.

The investigation missed horror.

Yet no one complained, preferring to imagine a pale language, paler than a linen tablecloth or the desert's unlit night.

Poe's white Baltimore stoop mounting to a door.

FORM

Nothing to ennoble the passion for measure and number, for the hard precincts of form, that uncanny love, surely as indictable as any great crime or gratuitous enormity.

Yet, with one's attention span, the mind wandered out, a weighted thing to be pushed forth on a cloud of moistened breath, to soar and curl itself about a street or a city.

Hungerings occurred amid the silted isobars of hope, in love's calms and tempests, sloughs of logic gone astray which had left us open to chance and to a desiring to persist.

The self's tellings were another moon haunting its own sublunary. It sought itself as a name high over soil it had made, rocks, cities, isolate worded beings.

MNEMOSYNE

O Mother memory, yes!

I had visited in Spain, did my Goya-walk to the nth, but it barely got me to Lorca.

The *duende*, mysterious visitor, came and went.

The dead war ravaged among villagers.

And suddenly the muse was no longer a headstone stippled with *palabras*.

THE LOCAL

Actually, by accident of birth, I was born to homelessness and nothingness.

Later I opted for the local, for the 63rd A.D. election district and its bands of refugees who vanguard at the doors to ATMs.

Also to what the city advertises, gunk or hair gel, the stickiness of lost meanings, of signs secured by ripped awnings, foreclosures on the dark, dry pavings of a night skittish with deaths.

Beyond words' portals, I was always turned back, a bewildered Orpheus, city gentleman to Eurydice, an Amphion who gathered up stones into another hell-heap.

And now I feel a bit sickness-haunted, peering at the ineffable from an alley.

OUR TIME

Media voices over-wash all, blurring the inevitable: Psyche's credit-card sorting of the selves into collectives.

From the great engarblement, words are lifted out, and, in the current lexicon, crowd aside columns of pictures, taking one past new literals for contemplation among metonyms of blank.

GHOST

I was thinking about memory again, writing its letter home.

Before she died, her face, her favorite objects, etc.

Breakfasts were sweet, even...

On the table, the plunged gold plate of the bell on a silver creamer.

Someone left a world in it, a layer of puddled whiteness resembling a page, viscous, absorbent, richer than the *néant* Mallarmé inscribed on.

NEVER ONE

Because it is almost sound, it was meant for sharing.

We watched together the sun pour in the window, motes of light on glass and wood.

Who was home to this homeless light?

Together we dreamt of transports, of residences as glints off mica-ed rocks, centerless sheens bouncing from the frozen lake.

One felt the very slightness of being, almost validity's dusting up.

Yet also love, which hid us from the fiction's glare.

Pointless to ask for the addressee of desire.

Or that the mind misspoke its sonic phantoms and conjured the self which erred and brought us to this place.

APHASIA

And now, the demiurge possesses a lightness, a wet nuzzling of hope blind to the part played by the geometer's art.

Bleached one, O muse, I think of you, your silences where the throat catches on emptiness, *that free flight into the wordless.*

O teacher, the sky's light is fading, and I have sought that one place, speechless to the moon, an omen blossoming at its own edge, a bizarre portraiture in the rush of things portentous.

Bleached one, what was strategy?

What was truth?

The plangent lucidity, the glass through which the light flowed.

In Paris

The Place de la République's outdoor cafe, white wine
in a glass so thin it blurs realms with the greenery,

and with a statue patina-ed bronze, its plaque too far to read,
dull-lettered, pigeon-marked, possibly a thesis on history.

Yet the student lesson for today was the bomb at Boulevard
St. Michel, and the tourist's heightened sense increased

in the evening's Semtex blast near Le Drugstore at L'Étoile.
Luxe, voluptuousness, the children of freedom have returned.

Benjamin was here in the late 1930s, jackboots down the
     street,
wrote to Scholem of his "estrangement from everyone he
     knew."

Old Paris, carnage and death, St. Denis grilled on the
     champs,
the slaughtered diners at Goldenberg's in the Marais. I have

eaten there too, and now the wine's tincture puckers the lips,
and then the buds of flavor burst coming through, like a life

passed from one into another's care, in the City of Light
where hope was stifled once between *le mot juste* and *le
     mot juif.*

Thinking of Mary

in memoriam, Mary Oppen, d. 1990

On the ride down to Carmel, as we talked,
the held-back feelings surged like the Pacific,
and suddenly a young girl's face broke surface.

I was seeing fifty years back, swerving
with the roadway into old stories:
the barge canals of France, Pound and Rezi,

time's acoustics on an odd headland like this,
sounding a way to the end of the century.
Then we left the car and walked on hilltops,

the bay spread off west, and to the east,
the Sierra's bluish haze. Your painter's eye
picked out the sights, weighing and measuring

the dry California light, the brown wiry grasses
ruffling. Later at Marie's, the tick of the pines
mingled with house talk: poems, art, Jeffers's Tor,

the harsh look you shot at those you'd barely suffer,
these were as balks for you against the age. The woods
outside were a paradise to the imperfect, the branches

fanning into wind streams. And that you judged—
frightening those near you—a sharpened knife to pare
out Mary, *not* the poet's wife. After George's death,

it struck me, you came into your own in your collages,
piecing sky-blue paper onto cloth until they belled out
with the continent's inhuman spaces. You moved from

the bedroom shared with him into a smaller space, futon
on the floor, as though recalibrating yourself. Perhaps
you were listening there for the new life growing, growing

back like a circle on itself or like the ocean's recurrent
     tidal sweeps,
scouring the present for the past until you were a child
again before loss and could begin at last your weeping.

Parents' Grave

To learn from what you do there,
under a mound, not even a mound
but the barely perceptible
rise in the earth.

To learn your now famished learning,
that the texts were no good for you,
the hand in its doings, the head full of play,
comic, but leaving the hunger you must leave.

All you hoped to accomplish by now.
And I put my head down to that ground, still
a child, instructed by what only you can teach,
a piece of the night fallen into it.

The old machine, time and place, where I put you both.
Tears which come. The new language, only translation.

One Day, What You Said to Yourself

Winter. Two trees in the yard of Friends Seminary
are without leaves, stark in their denudement.

The world glazed with cold, the homeless argue
in the park, their angry voices leaving them more naked.

The trees, the limbs of which held foliage, branch
and twig that winter freed, ride higher and higher,

angling into the sky and sun. But you had tired of
the bare data, the nictating perception which crowed

like a bird, *I live*, exuding the old lyric order of the world,
so that a corner was turned, the image bedded in stealth,

to emerge neither for nor against. Only some principle
you wanted without war or hope for life better than

a privileged fold in history such as the powerful make, rather
something just there in the interstices, call it a moment,

the fragment, the sweet taste of her in the second
person, for the record, later the ambush. You

encountered the trees and the trees met you and won.

She

is looking up, and then she is not looking up.
With a lovely uncontrollable quiver, she's become herself.

I can see she is no longer the breasts which offer up
their enticements, nor the dark mysteries of the pubis.

She is not even her laugh. She is she, without residuals.
'Bye, my love, I think. And, possibly, *by* my love? And I

am happy, happier even then when her mouth is on me
   and I
gasp at the ceiling.

Sag Harbor, Whitman, as if an Ode

I

And so again, to want to speak—as though floating on this
    world—
thoughts of Sagaponak, of Paumanok, "its shore gray and
    rustling,"

To remember late sun burnishing with a pale gold film
the feathery ghosts of blue heron and tern, of that same
    light

furrowed in the glyphed tracks to bay water. And at night,
to scrape one's own marks in sand, a bioluminescence
    underfoot

by which we playfully signaled, as the heat of bodies also
was a signal to turn to each other in the guesthouse
    buried

in deep-sunk must and trellised scents. As though, again,
    to be
as with mossed graves which, even as they lie under new
    buds,

are worn and lichened, chiseled over with letter and
    number,
entrapped, as in the scripts of museum words, *trypots* and
    scrims.

And so, like whalers, whose diaries record a lostness to
    the world

in the sea's waves, to find ourselves in talk's labyrinth
  where

the new is almost jargon, and we speak of lintels of a
  house
restored or of gods who stage their return at new leaf or
  where

pollen floats on water in iridescent sheens.

II

But also now, to sense mind harrowed in defeats of
  language,
Bosnia, Rwanda, wherever human speech goes under a
  knife.

And to be unable to look to the sea, as to some watery
  possibility
which would break down the hellish rock of history that
  rides

above wave height as above time. Strange then, these
  littorals
teeming with sea life, with crab and ocean swallow.
  Strange then,

to walk and to name—glad of that momentary affluence.
And so to find again the vibratory spring that beats against

old voicings, old silences, this waking to those fables
  where

new bees fly up, birthed spontaneously from the log's
    hollow,

to hear again the Latinate of returning birds keeping alive
curiosity and memory, as if the ear were to carry us across
    hope's

boundary, remembering the words: *Now, I will do nothing
    but listen!*

Exigent Futures (2003)

Cyclical

It was on that day when the Names were not,
Nor any sign of existence endowed with name.
                                        —Divani Shamsi Tabriz

I

I was remembering how the city took shape by the offices of light. How our words were lovely evensong, trilling above the muted rumble of buses, delicate, yielding, a kind of looseness twanging off the metallic forest of rooftops.

We had wormed ourselves down into darkness, descending, self-blinded air-moles, and then sun and memory rose, and our plangent mindfulness was godlike, a backing and filling which laid out the boulevards and crushed the sparrow.

At midday, a precision of shadows illumined the telltale refuse in the streets.

Love hectored: were we to exist, our *being* a kind of coruscation across the sallow air?

(So many machines, so much impelled movement. It was left to verbal mechanisms to draw down the power, to blow fuses, to irrigate the grid with nonsense syllables.)

II

It hurt to be invaded by our surpluses, to wander in that crowded yet lonely Gehenna, to ask who chose these spend-thrifts of architecture, these markings and commerce, the ornate cornices, spandrels, coffee machines and bottled water?

Amidst findings of anguish and lust, there was an immense betokening of intimacies threaded to the wrong objects.

The flux baffled, engarbled speech.

Yet still, a few stood proudly cut from the mechanics of illumination, their faces written upon by hopes and pains, singular and yet embossed by unplanned beginnings and ends.

They exhibited an uprightness, not of freedom, but rather as though a tree had resisted back against the brutal informing weathers of history, those mournful plenitudes, cares, bents, desires and redeemings.

The objects were now more ghostly, more unaccountable, and thus no longer those things about which banished rhapsodes were entitled to sing.

Meanwhile, the verse's flatness hinted at a tutelary linguistics, at an awareness of thought's barely inflected swiftness, of substance that left one both free and bereft.

III

Philosophers proclaimed the mental light as holding this *lumina, luxe.* But grime smudged against vision, smeared the sense of beauty with the prolix essences of markers.

The light, imageless, bathed real objects, fell across her brow and face, onto contours of small breasts, dark furtive sexual hairs...

Less personal, the light also slatted up the city into longish beam-work, Brownian fonts of godheads, their secondary power a kind of utterance.

IV

These dream states implied auroras of flooding radiance, offset the textures of the brickwork, traduced them into penetrant nostalgias of barred and indexed windows, dark homiletics of streets, the coarsened kelps of entanglement.

In spite of an overriding sense of packed and sectored prox- imities, emotion broke from one's fears, likewise the reverse, etc., occurring as though in the trued rooms of an abiding, momentous dwelling.

Or as fantasy suggested: a child walked down leafy lanes, embracing a storybook dappling, only to turn a corner, to emerge from the glade and come upon the concrete Behemoth itself.

Therefore that other fealty to the premonition that each word was not the dawn but a nailing sun at noon?

No shadow of ambiguity on the paving stones.

V

The calculus on the page, the numbers and symbols, the operands and constants, transparencies and theories. Only these thwart an interminable bruising against reason.

Morning's light had never been particularly confirmatory.

VI

Sun's faint warmth as yet not fully given over to the day's shape, still enmeshed in night.

Its light arrived and with it the wheeled traffic in the street.

Time, the indulgent parent...

As though the mind were primitive, a forest of deep recurrence in matted leaves and balsams of pine. Memory futile, grasping at technique again.

VII

And what was writing? *A snail's slime down the walkway!*
Nothing more natural to the creature, he wrote bitterly.

O and by the way, little soul, how is a cognizable world
possible?

Is it infarct or comestible?

Only yesterday, the old Printing House Square, buildings
torn down, resembled the site of a molar's extraction.

And this month, litter thickens to a matted surface catching
about the feet, to ankle-turning slipperiness of compacted
color supplements, the musical crackling of Styrofoam cups.

But you, you are positively beautiful, done in, or, as the
French say, *en déshabillé*.

Not a word for thought in this enjambed paradise of desires.

VIII

Evil more clear than good, wound more certain than caress—
the unloved always recognizable when posed against the
loved one who remains unknowable.

Face secreted in mystery, city's mystery.

What about one who lies athwart a darkness, stamped by incised verities?

Be wary of judgment, best to withhold closure on another.

Attention and skilled action, even these must suffer hesitancy. It was the only way we could talk about streets and neighborhoods, thinking where they blend or die off or transmute to something else.

The most opaque thing is the body which you peer down at as from a crown.

Thought's pinnacle?

Easy, however, to float off with the wave of a hand, a dream of oneness—her skin and freshets of eye contact, mouth or curves, the secret places.

Thus the ruminations and the trust, estranged valuations, the city coalescing as fragile web, the familiar trickling like an open tap into homelessness.

"We can only wish valeat quantum valere potest."

for A.S.

The dead were to be interrogated
beside the meaning "sign."

We looked in vain for the words
"cow," "sheep," "pig," etc.

Hahriya meant not only "to comb,"
but also to touch affectionately,

to stroke, to caress, to fondle—
also to tickle and incite,

(and in the sexual sense, to be
caught in the dreams of *Puduhepa*).

On many days, we admonished
ourselves for our arrogance.

Much of the vocabulary consisted
of words hidden behind logograms,

indicative of first things,
the need and desire to speak,

to bring back the body. Thus,
who to propose a given meaning,

who to vouchsafe its reliability?
The dead did not need our wisdom.

One context would have allowed the idea
"to hurl, to shoot," another "to dismiss,

to throw, to push aside (as a child)."
The word stems were clearly uncertain.

In the documents, *eribuski*, the eagle
was made of gold, and flew over

without conjecture. But *elwatiyatis*,
with its many syllables, meaning unknown,

appeared again and again in connection
with the word for "billy goat."

Questions remained. The void offered utterance.
We thanked the impenetrable silence for permission,

for deepest gratitude. We bowed to
the acrid muteness of another world.

Take *esarasila* (the context does not
give meaning), but we pondered its sound

on air, for we had been given the word as though
incised in stone, as glyph or diadem, as memorial.

Esharwesk translated, not only as *"blutig machen,
mit Blut beschmieren,"* but "to become, to turn red."

Layers were many. And here, face it, we sought
another's breath, mother to our language.

We sought sound as resurrection. With this,
we were *beschmieren*. The gold eagle flew

toward a reddened sky, the word stem not always clear.
But better to not have attempted the translation?

Halkestaru, "Watch, night watch," was actually
two words. Difficult to have taken any of this

as causative. Still, all we wished for
was that our efforts be *harnuwassi*,

"of the birth stool," or that we would be led
to *hantiyara*, a place in the riverbed where fish live,

a "backwater." *O Valeat quantum valere potest.*
No work for the self, only lust for lost voices,

fellow *hapkari* (pairs of draft animals)...

Autobiographia

Weren't you given a text? To honor the congregation, the
    organ dulcet,
the cantor's hum, hymnal of Europe's East, steps of sound
    made fugal

but laden with a weariness (joy for another day), history
    transmogrified
into plaint upon plaint, to be ushered into manhood, to be
    brought other's pain.

Early on, the *Shekhinah* gone into exile. Most of that
    century you saw
not love but power, cruelty, the face which laughs against
    the sun.

What could you do if you were not steeped in things like
    the others
but merely walked to buy milk or bread, heaven above,
    earth below,

to visit the old streets, the elm's grainy seeds lying across
    paving stones,
tourists milling and the Atlantic past the bridge brilliant
    as a sword cut.

Saline, solute, salve, this art burning to base metal. What
    carries one
who would sing a hymn but eddies of language—never the
    pure thing—

maelstroms and tidal pools, word forms, the will hemmed in like an ocean
to its basin, rhymed to the rack of its tides. The word's ring deflected

in the baffles of the city into space, echo bounced from storefront to tower,
fading toward soundlessness—ear cupped to catch emptiness, translation

to Paradise from which speech fled. *Put down this cloth, said the rabbi.*
Cover the text and emplace the cap. Live neither in blacks nor whites.

Avert from the scroll rising above the earth, gaze upon limitless blue,
the inventive weaving of clouds. Live straight ahead. Appearance

will be your pain and mentor. Be at the threshold, not at the Ark.
And later, to go back to plucking a word from the weave,

lamé, silver, deep magenta, designs mazed over the fold, lines and margins,
and underneath, as though one sensed through flesh, the delicate structure

of *beths* and *vavs* on parchment, the inner and outer of secrets.

Winter Notes, East End

to Armand Schwerner, in memoriam

Finding the nothing full, I bring myself back
to the day's page, the window's revealing expanse

of snow, *bardos* tamped down upon *bardos* (*it is not
possible to contract for a stay*), brittle leaves

which sign but do not speak, the frost, the graveyard
across the road leaking its supply of portents, jargons

of elegies, white words without issue, the swan
on thin ice, images which imbue, only to lend perfume
to the acrid taste of being countried outside a soul.

◆

At midnight, Orion and the Dog Star swell in blackness.
And on clouded nights, no constellation and no
    consolation.

Intelligence unable to code another winter night which,
    like
a tunnel, leads back to a helplessness only a child should
    feel.

◆

At the window, January's sparse glories:
ice crystals adhering to rocks,

also winter birds that never quite
belong in snow-struck landscapes—

they signal what burns up old mechanisms,
the rote cyclicals of seasons, routines

into which one-way time-bound bodies are cast.
Winter making one desire—that part of it

containing stars or blankets, anything memory
clings to or words rend open. Stagnant water

reflecting back ridges of heaped-up ground.
An autumnal reflux embodying a sorrow

or hunger for unfixed space. Death imagined
as a motionless mode of contemplation.

◆

This world, that—I know one
should stop. Tired eyes

should rise from inked blue
lines inscribed on yellow pad.

And that the eye should elect
this hovering blur which,

if one is tired enough, becomes
spectral green as though

through writing one came
again to a parkland.

◆

Do you trust phenomena? Old literalist,
Blake's guinea sun is mocking you.

These short days blend unawares into nights,
instructions in how to join the great poets.

O yon pillowed laughter! Yet somewhere,
a dog howls, and self-knowledge is suddenly

the heat of an immense banked fire. Gone now,
names sequent to things unnamed. The blank page

no mystery. Composition is, composition is...

♦

Philosopher's stone, shrine room's hoardings.
Everything under the august calm of the sacred.

Still panic that one can't live to the smallest jot,
to the least syllable of the matter. Wasn't it called

ghost or haunting, an iota of someone left?
Remember the dead or must a kind of *iotacism*

be proposed? Homer long ago: each beat
of the line awash in Heraclitus's river.

♦

Scouring words for the relieving aura,
breathing deeply old vocabularies of sea,

of pine, ever-present tinge of salt.
Panoply of stars, planets. But often

one can't find what is being searched for,
the galaxy seemingly drained of that covenant.

Thus is it written out for syntax's rules,
for the untranslatable memory of black holes,

for voice, for love and against concept.

Eschaton (2009)

On a Phrase of Milosz's

> *He is not disinherited,*
> *for he has not found a home*

He has found vertiginous life again, the words
on the way to language dangling possibility,

but also, like the sound of a riff on a riff,
it cannot be resolved. History has mucked this up.

He has no textbook, and must overcompensate,
digging into the memory bank if not for the tune

then for something vibratory on the lower end of the
    harmonics.
He's bound to be off by at least a half note—here comes
    jargon

baby—something like a *diss* or hiss. Being is
incomplete; only the angels know how to fly homeward.

Yet, once the desperate situation is clarified, he feels
a kind of happiness.

◆

Later, the words were displaced and caught fire, burning
    syllables
to enunciate the dead mother's name.

(*Martha* sounding then like "mother")

Wasn't it such echoes that built the city in which he lives,
the cage he paces now like Rilke's panther?

He was not disinherited.

He was not displaced

He is sentimental; hence he can say a phrase like *his heart burst*

The worst thing is to feel only irony can save

The worst thing is to feel only irony.

My City

This constellation is a name
before words

no god has a hand here,

and distillates of memory

crystallize then reveal
structural flaws

unplanned as cells
gone wild in a tumor

Possibly, the bird
was once an eagle

but now a mourning dove
coos on the window ledge,

abandons its two white eggs
to the pigeon or the peregrine

The hole in the downtown
sky is of another order,

purchased from the fractals,

made one with the incalculable
past tense about to conjugate a future

Diasporic Conundrums

Call me not Naomi, call me Mara —Ruth 1.20

And now this man is fatherless
because he had a father,
and Israel is no more.

A line encircles
deserts beyond Jerusalem,
and he who was given a name
has lost the right to silence.

The man had a mother
because he had a mother,
and Israel never was.
Jerusalem, city's mirage,
shimmers on desert sands.

How could this be real?
Who will rise up
a name like Ruth,
put a name,
like a child, onto the air?

The dead are dead.
This is certain.
This is what was written,
why it was written.
This need not be said.

Bandelette de Torah

In honor of the Eternal One, it has been made,
this band and cloak, by the young and dignified girl,
Simhah, daughter of the cantor, Joseph Hay, son
of the wise and noble Isaac.
      —Musée d'art et d'Histoire du Judaïsme, Paris, 1761

The hunger is for the word between us,
between outside and in, between Europe
and America, between the Jew and his other,
the word and the non-word.

In the museum case, belief has been sealed
behind glass. The gold *Yod*, fist-shaped
with extended finger, marks where the letter
is made free, *davar* twining *aleph* into thing.

The hunger was once for textured cloth, brocade
of thread, gold-webbed damask, tessellate fringe,
for sewn-in weight of lead or brass, the chanter
lifting all heaviness from the page, singing out

lost richness. He followed the gold *yod* of divining,
alchemic word intoning the throne's measure in
discarded lexicons of *cubits* and *myriads*. The cloth
lay over Europe's open scroll between Athens and
    Jerusalem,

between library and dream. What if Athens were to be
entered only via the syllogism or Jerusalem's sky
were written over in fiery labyrinth, in severe figures,
unerring texts? The hunger was for the lost world

that lay between Jerusalem and Athens. Later, terrors
came to be its portion, flames beyond remonstrance,
synagogue and worshiper in ash. Celan in the Seine
with its syllabary. The words were as burls in woven cloth.

They lie across the lettered scroll, ink on paper
enveloped in darkness, desperate to be inmixed
with matter. The words were between us, poised
to rise into constellated night as task unto the city,

to enter *this* place unshielded between the One
and nothingness, if only to exist as from an echo
between hope and horror, between sacred sound
and profane air. Between Athens and Jerusalem and
    America.

The Chronicle Poet

One tries pulling syllables clean, like freeing
old nails from plaster. Undoing the dismantling of
human gantries by listening, as though one had an empty
water glass to his ear, wondering about the other side,
shushing wife, child, visitor, the gnawing of a rat,
to catch sounds between these histories and our
    apartments.

What is overheard is mere scratching, someone perhaps
short of air, desperate, a man eating dictionaries
quickly, avidly, hopelessly. Useless, useless! Nothing
impedes thought's passage more than an unuttered word,
one desperately cut short or untimely enough to have
    become stuck
where it makes only a shameful noise, a beetle's endless
clicking in the throat of a corpse. A noise seeking to reach
its fundament, trying, out of pure sound, to form itself
as honest language, and by that failure, painfully
    embarrassing.

Four London Windows

ON KENTISH TOWN ROAD

Breakfast by the cafe's window when sound truck
blared "Jesus is Hope"; old madrigal twanged
by guitar and fiddle. Feedback from speakers

echoing off crumbling brick to spike that piety
with the present. And, while drinking coffee,
a young, still-singing girl, dispatched from

the marchers, hands him a flyer block-lettered:
PEACE and HOPE. Then suddenly, to hear talk of
business in the City, of changes in the price of stocks

as they shuffle across a screen, giving out their unmeant
meanings: who to be clothed, who fed; in what wars, what
color would the people be running from fiery villages.

So much like a music which lightly touches a world,
bulked and muffled in laminates of history. And so,
the stillness when the girl has left. No word

to pierce that plane of glass, and this to carry
on his walk to the Underground, the procession
alongside him in the street. Song, music, earnestness.

He descends to the Northern line and out at Camden Town
catching again the marchers' shouted "No" to the world,
walking amid the crowds, parting that sea of resigned faces.

LONSDALE SQUARE

is perfect now, but wasn't this what the Victorians
wanted us to be, living under that perfected row
of rooftops serrate under skies, a god's knife in ascent

to jigsaw the world into its proper places. Also,
the little park is perfect—a squared-off ambuscade
that shut out the grime of mills, the young girls sold

under the railway bridge. In Lonsdale Square now,
the windows tell no truths. Fine dinner glass, they merely
hold the clouds. One looks through to neat walled yards.

SOHO

Sex shop's open window box is curtain fringed.
I hear her say "lovely" as I go past, quick
peer down hallway tinged with pastel light.

She's young enough to make one gasp, to buy
one's self from time. The curtain strips
comb out against the air. Shot silk; no glare.

The light and forms too difficult, too obscure.
But see back to Hagar and to Sarah who stand
sphinxlike at these windows to the future.

WESTMINSTER

Silence heavy as the stones covering poets and kings.
And light, a fine wash of water and flour, spills down.
We and other tourists afloat in it, disembodied

in the pews, untethered from carpeted aisles. *Unreal city—*
its vague hum muffled in high vaulted rafters. Blake,
honored in the Corner. *Man is either Ark of God or*
    phantom

of the earth and of the water. Here all is prophecy and
    trance.
We are such baffled languages now: is a word any more
than a window open to a space halfway between us?

Mortise and book, leaded lattice, love and body.
What is uttered, the seen movement of another's lips,
    brings
the mirror down, opens a transept to quickened
    transparency.

Like Prose Bled Through a City

Yes, I have followed them, time and again! —Baudelaire

THIRD AVENUE

It was lovely—exeunt clouds, but I turned
        the corner, just today, to see the man
facedown on the sidewalk, a model for some
        bas-relief, a thick grime impacted
into his skin and clothes, he had made it halfway
        to some kind of stone.

Possibly, in my mind, he was already assuming
        an icon's status, a little figure in a niche
which flares in the caught light on walls.
        Certainly, I wanted him exemplary, easing
the disparity that opened between us
        to remind me that the language must be clear today
and show its encumbrances, the unintended beads
        of utterance that catch meaning out of sorts,
as if to say, desperately, "beautiful days, clear days,
        exuberant days, days of light of the late
city's century."

IN ROY ROGERS

This woman takes up a lot of physical space with four
        shopping bags filled with her scores
from garbage pails. She is going by me, cutting
        a swatch out of the neutral air as though
she were mere nothing, a bit of my eye's saccade,
        my city eye moving decisively and furtively...

And only this iris's flicker discloses the flawed
        ratios between the physical and the mental,
as it also works in reverse, in my head with
        its minor headaches, the harassments of
finding a minor thing "too much" one day, so
        pulling back as she goes by or I go past

and then trying to analyze that guilt-prowed surge
        as though the ripple of me had pushed
the spar—once again—from her reach,
        naturally, seen from the viewpoint of the spar.

EITHER, OR, BUT

Nervous, with fear and trembling (*either*
I've drawn down Kierkegaard into this riff,
or I've not). But the sky was very blue today,
and across it only a few clouds made their way,
buttressing against the west, almost stately
as though a language of forms resided there.

That the gods should be lodged in the sky!
Forcing the eyes to rise from the street,
to look at the immense unspeakable silence.
But—and every word very much hangs on a but
these days—I was drawn by the sounds of a man
and a woman arguing while a small boy
with squinting eyes, frightened, looked
at this one and then at that—as though
one were the sky and one were the street.

I've drawn Kierkegaard into this work
because of his Abraham in terror under
the desert sky, on his way to Mirah
with Isaac in tow. Because of the child,
eyes moving, as ours, from street to sky.

Creeks in Berkeley

You who cannot love a freely spoken word
find delight in these half-enclosed rills
where bittercress and wild lily mat
and so cover the sharp-edged enclosing stone
muffling the water's musical notes
as they blend or accompany the voice
heard on the street or enter barely noticed
into homes edging the small open spillways
before the water slips under cemented rock
to travel beneath streets, its force
lost at sea level where it flows from outlet
upon outlet flattening into the bay's wide expanse.

You led yourself or were you led by her who once
lived on Cragmont and whose voice has its own sweet
rill running uphill with a freedom teasing you
from any turn or enjambment until sound disappears
into the air, into a wordless breathing of light
the late sun strikes from the bridges and the windows.

At Word-Brink

I alone, featherbedded in language.
I alone, luxuriant in speech,

How to put world there, at word-brink
among so many lovely things that flow?

Who to claim otherness in flesh,
in love-tinged landscapes? I alone.

Remembering old unbridgeable sadness.
Unable to put the case. And who,

if not I, to mourn for lost parents,
for Michael who must mourn?

In the loose talk of language,
that omnivore, so much are these

estrangements no longer
of the glib morning of novelty.

What to come of time stringing words' syntax,
inscribing us together? *I alone*,

that closed bell ringing homonym sound
of another word, isle or island.

A Dialogue of Some Importance

One's hand. Its whole existence.
Minuscule things it seeks to grasp.

> *the hand that moves to touch,*
> *lost by the mind before it moves,*
> *so who propels it thus?*

Her nipple. A crumb. The furled edge of a tissue.
Surely there is some charm to rolling bread
into small resilient balls, casting them off
the fingertips to squawking ducks.

> *is it only an emissary,*
> *a move of a heart in flight,*
> *to mark where, in outward scenery,*
> *it seeks to lodge itself?*

Often, I am swamped by incredible pleasure,
by the wild connection a thing makes between
my thumb and finger, as though desperately alive
in some galvanic dance. *Ouroboros* tastes his own tail,

> *self-love? love's self?*
> *who guides a hand knows*
> *the horror of attached.*

but I have made deities
out of the lint of carpets,
metallic granules and snotballs,
especially out of lost eyeglass screws.

Exercise on Schiele's
Die Junge Frau

Sight is like water
        which to the leaf won't cling.
Yours is a young girl's thighs and ass.

I am related
        as rain-soaked to stone.
The self is what waits.

Searing shapes have been torn
        from ancient forms.
Never mind that mother suckled the past

nor that father mapped days ahead.
        The self is what waits,
and you are a hope lodged in time's interstices.

Seeing alone invents.
        Breasts high, shirt
sails from head and arms, a thrown-off banner

by which the eye's
        conqueror makes her jest.
The self is what waits.

Homan's Etchings

MAPLE

Here, the paper's plane
by which one enters a mysterium
to find foregrounded
before the trunk, a branch.

And where on paper
did the burin's point touch down,
why voice over voice
and why each leaf must overlay a leaf?

Paper's edge—
growth   nothing.

ANEMONE

A sea of leaves stroked in
—different leaves—
rioting out of the same core.
Say again: sea of leaves,
trembling with the wind, *anemos*.
I speak for my own comfort. Say again.
I speak anemone *bosanemoon*,
the faint wavering,
the silk of the words.

BRETAGNE

What came first? The ruined house
shows humankind was here, the fence post
placed upright. Far off, the church's steeple.
In close, high grass one almost feels
as though walking to the crumbling brick.

Under that broken roof, the curious story:
What came first. And how it came
to entwine the wire with the rose.

TAK ESDOORN (diptych: maple branch split by seam)

O bud, on the other side!
O parent, O child!

GEESE

Etched brambles and flat light,
and nearly too cold and brilliant
to look, to raise one's head
above the rise, the nearby stark
entanglings that form
a delicious aftersex, the drug,
that puts off winter.

                                    And so,

the distant flock rises
almost imperceptible to mind,
to wheel and turn, to fade in cloud ...
unless there is a witness,
a ceremonial: a word.

AUTUMN

to Homan

You have invited me to die
by ripe entertainments, so I
make a horse's head
of fungus-crusted stump
and gaze with dead eyes
of a dog where a great
branch broke from the tree.
I count patches of lichen,
enumerate their missing tints.
Each bit of lined decay
must be imagined, eye
made surfeit with its true
entangling: dead log,
sinuous vine, thorn and bract.
Autumn. Gone is syntax.

Report on the Dispatches

words of reason drop into the void —Simone Weil

REPORT

And then they[1] brought the receptors up.
One saw soldiers[2] who were standing, looking
frightened before the endless troughs of sand.

Grainy films of grit and oil clung to lenses
as though inert, in the dead voice of matter's
humming,[3] was calling out for company with inert.

Below encodings of the tongue, the trembling halts
and stutterings had been prioritized, first in the queues
of abject sounds made incommensurable[4] and then
    repeated.

Such wordless brilliances—the automated incunabula
of the synapse—lay pooled in adrenal shallows below
language's hard unyieldings, blighted by fearweeds,

which took sounds and made them narcotic. And when one
finally spoke, webbed into circuits with other warriors,
each word was presumed wedded to its proximate word

as though signaling[5] a commonality that would flash
through other shuttered apertures—say ears—
say passages normally closed off from light.

1. THEY—This collective "they" lived nowhere, camping out in front of the barbed-wire gates of the base or on the remote fringes of the battlefield, an enormous heliotrope swinging its vast head toward unimaginable stimuli, amalgams of anguish and violence. As the senior members of the profession chanted "Accuse me, I am old, and I am a part, accuse me," their aloneness was assuaged, their solitude was banked. The reporter's eye no longer looked for data but sensed a focus, some prominence as the sun flared or the night flared and assumed momentary shape.

2. SOLDIERS—The soldiers' lovely naïveté: sweet limbs, some marking their uniforms with odd patches and flags, offering up to the bloody-mouthed gods, their individuation, even as they approached death in the trenches. This horror.

3. MATTER'S HUMMING—Unwordable or unsayable "humming," such as that which preexists on magnetic tape, the bass note of the Western canon. Subject to entropy, it lacks sufficient energy to sustain itself, to prevent decay and therefore, by the most violent means, finds, ultimately, an external force (an enemy) to enable its vivification.

4. SOUNDS MADE INCOMMENSURABLE—Without measure and having no meaning, hence no limit—mere utterance aimed at the other side of disaster, hence hopelessly and solely self-reflective, something like the exegesis of one's own death rattle.

5. SIGNALING—Socrates, in warning against the effects of poetry, describes it as an overwriting or inscribing upon "the city within oneself." In times of war, however, there is a

secondary function, a kind of ghostly telling, often too late to be heard, amounting to a sort of compromised message between a man and his corpse.

Sarajevo and Somalia

Beauty is such a magnet, the art world such a thief,
the paintings sit in the galleries of the present
sucking up the real, like mirrors for the chosen.

The poems are for the unelect, for those who discover
that words have been ransacked. Surely, the more one reads,
the more one feels a word is unable to resist paying its
    ransom.

This was yesterday: "I want to describe what I saw, a rib
    cage
starved to bone." And something terribly linguistic about
literalness has escaped to wander among other phrases

such as: "rib-eye steak" or "chew my bone." And these,
the broken bona fides of our speech, nomad memory
and pitch tents of poetry on abandoned ground.

The Assumption

after a painting by Paula Rego

How else does the mother rise
      but on baby Jesus's back?

Ask his mother, he looked like an angel,
      he was an angel

Before his virgin birth,
      before Mary was even a mother.

Precariously, her head is thrown back.
      Looking up? Loss of balance?

No matter what, the boy will be burdened
      with going down to earth,

With his agony, and with his rising up.
      Already the worry lines show

In his young face. Great weights are
      first carried from and then to

A god on a wing flap. Every task
      is done at least twice.

In Irons

Our forebears observed rituals
of handheld tools, of the seamed
carpentry of open boats, the beauty
of waters and of compassed charts.

And from shallows, from near-to-shore sloughs
a few wandered into open sea where the eye
shaped new referents out of wave and cloud,
to save the mind from its aloneness.

And without meaning, the salt tear corroded,
water burned on cracked skin,
the current's hold on the craft was self-
canceling in the suppressed null of the seas.

There too the tongue turned under
as though one dropped an anchor
into unformed memory, watery, adrift,
looking into the black sea for a reflection
surfacing with the force of language.

Le Dernier Portrait

The matter of no longer having to speak and having no one nor anything to speak to. A matter of death masks in the Musée d'Orsay. Made by one who lays the gauze over the corpse's face and pours the clay and sips coffee while it sets. When what sets is the horror of the world, of the *not-you*, and what is left is this object imprinted with your features. *Ars longa*—the day's rictus. The absurd cheating because one's last day is never even a whole day. And here's this hardened object with its painted flesh tones, the pale, lightly brushed reds, beady fakery of glass eyes. Here in a museum, though this is hardly the time to suggest there's life in the thing, even if it's keeping august company with robust Maillols and Rodins. And with money and with the grand café whose tall windows bring Paris, gorgeous Paris, close enough to touch.

Everything homes toward these frozen visages. Here's Pascal, lidded eyes, dour expression without complacency for his century. Marat and Napoleon, so popular in death, they suffered five impressions each.

And what of those who leave no artifact but this, who are only this artifact, and that by chance?

La femme inconnue, a sort of Venus of this city. She threw herself into the river in a simple dress. The mask shows her smiling. Did she sense that she did not belong to Paris's well-tended streets? She inhabited that other side where the unnoticed poor go, *arrondissement*s of ruin and shame.

She never belonged, though there must have been moments

of half living, of half dying while she mermaided the Seine. She floated under the famous bridges, under their blackened barrel vaults. They were the wreaths of her cortege. She offered and was an offering to those lustrous waters, to a silence of enfolding depths, to the matter of having no one to speak for her.

Stanzas Without Ozymandias

Who finds the pedestal finds the poem.
To know time had its ruins, its knowledge.
The traveler was fortunate.

And now sand has its texts, its mica
and feldspar, its fulgurites and beaded quartz.
The heart a display case, the eye a catchment.

Granules adhere to fire-drawn surfaces,
mineraled and glassine—acolytes of the grain
fused to a speech of unwarrantable sermons.

Wind and lightning storms roll the high dunes
into long trenches, into tides of erasures, now
smoothed to a nothingness—an abyss for the geometer

who mourned the mirror's lack, who hungered for stars
hidden in the dark behind the day's brightness.
Hard to remember what tribes wandered with Moses

or even who invoked that sere alchemy when Jesus
    disappeared
for the numbered days of an older Flood, or what tempted
the saints to sit in their aloneness at the ledge? Unawares,

the bush burned, and the mirage shimmered. Solitude of
    those
who entered, who sought earthly want, though they
    wandered
in the skull of an angel, in the trepanned and bleached
    spaces,

remembering only the colorless semblances of their
   desires.
So now to place a word on it, like a bit of mica
winking in the sun. And now to place time on it,

as though time were the handwriting of the object's
   moment.
Effacement in the grammar impelling one to be only a
   shadow.

Eschaton

I don't know where spirit is,
outside or in, do I see it or not?

Time turned the elegies
to wickerwork and ripped-up phone books.

All that worded air
unable to support so much as a feather.

◆

If there's hope for a visitation,
only the ghosts of non-belonging will attend.

And now death is slipping back
into the category of surprise.

I sit up at night and pant, fear
half-rhyming prayer—

self beshrouding itself
against formlessness.

In-breath; out-breath.

Aria of the rib cage equaling apse.

Skull, the old relic box.

Ordinariness of the Soul

the dead
who gave me life
give me this
our relative the air

When I visit
here,
I feel as if
I stand apart,

apart at any city block,
but especially one
near a hospital
where the hurt
and bedraggled mingle,

where they talk
and bum cigarettes
and banter.
Any city block
makes me ask:

for whom ought
the muse to be real?
Or is her tomb
bare, and with
an empty coffin

(as though someone
swept up words,
bagged them for the media).

         Does it obtain—note,
I have to ask in *legalese*?

For whom
         is the world's desire
to make real its desires?
         As though underneath
an impulse

a profounder
         truth were met,
not in grief
         but from a need
to find someone

and their wants,
         to find
one's companions.
         as they mingle.
To sense

         they too make
this same pilgrimage
         when they visit here,
standing apart.

An Interpellation

And now, they clamor
for masterpieces to burn

desperate to send up into air
the ash of Racine or the Bard,

to watch it drift down as prose
on those still listening. But I need

to talk about those works
one reads endlessly over the dead,

those slowly turned pages, half hope
and half hubris, to speak in favor of the classics

of living up to them, as though one
could rise on the wind from a worded grave

with the taste of cinders in the mouth.
No other way to make a life of ruminant memory

but by piecing out uncertainty's frightening ellipse
even as this condemns the mind for a moment

to the thoughts of others. No other way
but to be awakened to another language, to return

to a voice haunted by unknowing, to the dead's
unfilled fantasies of hope or love, to those words

capped now by finality, by a closure that cuts off
their sounds and makes an ashen sky look wider and
richer.

The Age of the Poet

What are the book's pages
            meant for?
The world is played out,
            and mind seeks its high,

a throne above care—
            not for blessing,
though it might come to that,
            but for surcease, for stillness,

for not thinking. Dog of a poet,
            bones of words, having lost
for this age the sweetness
            of referent—Rilke the last to say

house, home, tree?
            (knowing our time demands
cold invention,
            that tepid faculty-room tea.)

No way to find oneself,
            unable to wish exile.
And always belonging
            in a wronged way.

One face, the coin of alienation,
            the other smiling as if to pay
the due bill of self-image.
            Creature of the mind-screen.

Preferences, apathy and boredom?
        Managed fate?
You inscribed yourself, then lived
        as a beggar irritated by those

whose emotions ran unchecked,
        who gave themselves
to false gods, to the idea
        of an impotence authored by others.

Letter and Dream of Walter Benjamin

Messiah and geography never coincide.

After the Fall, the only bliss was silenced nature.
It reeked of the sadness of uninscribed creation.

The slow erasure of Torah's black letters,
written Law isolate amidst whiteness.

Paradises of language ought to reign,
celebrations of rising from mute space,

from infinity's ground, all the unknowable names.

◆

These, as I strolled, were my contemplations.

Swans were rising from the pond in the park.

And yes, I might have longed instead for vanished reflections,
for disappearing ripples left behind.

For now, I am reduced to sending you these eighteen pages
that muse on the horrible present—on our politicians, those
hastily put-up men, who garner for themselves the laurels
of the state.

They too have created infinities, blind alleys, endless mon-
uments to iniquities, a multitude of pains for others to bear.

They will outlive their brief immortality and leave a grubby ration of murderous hopes.

So imagine me moving amidst clouds of dust under a mountain of books, not to Palestine but to another of Berlin's forbidding streets.

Wiping clean the unpacked books.

They will sit on their shelves as we await fearful marching in the street, boots stamping over their pages, coarse shouts, frenzied thought...

Impossible for me to write of other topics, mathematics and language or mathematics and Zion.

The only path, these days, my bitter words.

I do recite the litany you imparted to me.

First things: unriddle Kabbalah.

Unriddle text.

But the truth is, I found myself reading the despair I find everywhere inscribed in this city.

Messiah and geography never coincide.

◆

He climbed a labyrinth,
a labyrinth of stairs,
past other stairways
descending.

He climbed
a labyrinth of stairs,
each step tested
with his foot.

Always tentative,
always hopeful,
while nearby,
other stairs descended.

Breathlessly
he rose,
up to their heights. Chest aching,

thoughts twisting
between his temples,
head pounding
with his blood.

He felt light-headed,
fearing always
each step
would carry him
into the thinning air.

◆

"...and furthermore, the law's appearance should be the result of the knowledge of good and evil."

"...all visible law is law-making violence."

"Only the law of God or of the General Strike can undo the violence of this bloody law."

I am walking, not knowing whether the heart is full.

Not knowing whether the soul is full.

I would like to keep silent.

My eye registers tree, cloud, pavement.

Messiah and geography never coincide.

Commentary Is the Concept of Order for the Spiritual World

If these streets, this world,   are the arena,

then each person passed,   each bidding building

unentered, leaves room   for ruminations

illumined by an edge,   a backlit otherness

positing a liberty   to think or not think

an idea, to fly up   outrageously

or swoop earthward,   toward a grand passion

with a hawk's fierceness,   talons extended,

and yet, for a second,   to hesitate—

If we are always outside   the precincts of power,

even our own,   and so imagine

(for instance)   the possibility of a tyrant,

helpless for a moment   before sunlight's brilliance

on rolling grass,   if we no longer

keep to our assigned faith   as Job's messengers,

each escaped alone   *to tell thee*,

then the deep flaws,   the salvaging uncertainties

in the world's   overriding syntax—

love of self, for instance,   migrating to love of another—

or those records   of an observing eye

noting the lichen's patch   on the rock face,

the water's slow   eroding of the boulder,

(such witness   an ongoing work

of resistance),   wouldn't this proclaim

that *he is most apt   who brings with himself*

the maximum   of what is alien—

a sense of world-depths   that no longer crowd the mind,

thus a rich compost   of the literal

of what is said.

And then might not   our words loom

as hope against fear   for near ones,

for their gesturing   towards a future?

*Beckmann Variations
and Other Poems* (2010)

Into the Heart of the Real

—*Abtransport der Sphinxe (Removal of the Sphinxes)*, 1945

The Sphinxes have beautifully outlined breasts, and they stand proudly on their taloned feet. And their taloned feet rest proudly on stone pedestals. Wood for crates is stacked nearby, and a sister bird has taken flight. Each Sphinx, from its platform, tells a seductive tale. Each one makes a liar out of one of the others. Whether on the pediments of stone or placed for shipment on the tumbrels, they insist on whispering silky words in one's ear. Little breezes are stirred by their sibilant words, little swirls that are worse than typhoons or tornadoes. Big storms, hurricanes are the exhalents of the world's turning, of massive pressure gradients at the poles, knocking down buildings and flooding streets. But the tiny voices of the Sphinxes enter through the ears like silkworms; each weaves a gummy dream to the bones of the skull as though it were a shadow on the wall of Plato's cave. Each tiny voice blends in with the sound of the real, urgent, unappeasable. There's an official monitoring each skull who, even as he listens, is already insisting on the dream's removal. The Sphinxes must be carted off. One thinks that the officials would organize deliveries of this nature in secret or at least elsewhere, but no, I have seen each one at the embarkation point eagerly straining on a rope, gleaming with sweat, pulling the crates toward the outgoing barges.

Orders

—*Luftballon mit Windmühle*
(Air Balloon with Windmill), 1947

The order of the profane assists the coming of
a messianic kingdom, despoiled of gods.

No act of the saint equals autumn's rotting leaves.
No autumn compares to lovers trapped in their cage

nor to the tutored souls lashed to the vanes of turning
    windmills.
All circle between heaven and hell.

The air transmits their stories, their cries.

But the background is as of the immemorial sea—black
    waves, tinged by green
globe encircling, enframing the lawful and the boundless.

Falling Man

—Abstürzender (Falling Man), 1950

It is great to fall, it will be important if I plunge
this way, as it would not be great to be entangled.

But if I plunge head down, feet clear and don't catch
on a building ledge, I will swoop past the structure

blazing in flames on my right, go past the open window
to my left where one sees some compact of love, violent

and contorted, is acted out. I admit, it is great to fall, great
not to fear snagging on the buildings to the right or to the
    left,

wonderful to fall free from clouds swirled in turbulence,
passing toward the blue of the sea where a small boat
    sails,

where gulls fly like avenging angels, and the momentous
    inevitable
wheel of life and death has a benign dusty shine. I am
    going down,

dropping toward the cannibal plants, the cacti and Venus
    flytraps,
unnameable greens and jaundiced yellows. Down.

Triptych

—Argonauten (The Argonauts), 1949–50

THE WALL IT WILL HANG ON

He was born Diomedes, but a centaur renamed him,
so then he was Jason to Pelias, the king who feared him
because, as Pelias's dreams warned, beware the one who
wears only one sandal, and this is how Jason came to court.

And Pelias, rather than kill the young Jason on the spot
(the boy's relatives were in attendance), said to him, "Go
to Colchis for the ram's fleece." Pelias knew those masses
of gold curls were guarded by a monster who never sleeps.

Pelias was also haunted by Phrixus's ghost. Poor Phrixus
rode the wild ram to escape being made human sacrifice
by Orchomenes. Poor, dishonored Phrixus. When he died,
his corpse lay unburied, its ghost yearning for its body.

To lift the curse this deed cast, Pelias needed corpse and
    fleece.
And if by chance, Jason succeeded...well, it would go well
for Pelais either way. So Jason built the *Argo*. His crew,
those heroes who would later spawn a thousand myths.

Also he took on board women. Among them, rage-carrying
    Medea
and at least one invisible, interfering goddess who whispered
into Jason's ear words about fate, honor and the glories of
    the future.

RIGHT PANEL

All we are sure of is the chorus.
No single voice can sing as loud.
Frail ones empowered—thin staves
bundled with others to gain in strength.

Now unafraid, the small-minded
utter warnings and imprecations
or make a chorus of strident music,
notes stitches honor to mass identity.
Lute, pan pipe, hidden drum, voices
erasing doubt. The songs will make
the heroes do anything, will foretell
how it ends, will say hope lies in the journey.

LEFT PANEL

The woman (Medea?), poised with sword,
sits on the death mask of a head she has lopped off.

The bearded artist paints her as he would a violent king.

CENTER PANEL

An old man climbs the ladder from the sea.
Jason, beautiful boy, and Orpheus, lute at rest
upon the *Argo*'s deck, are gazing at each other.

The bird of wisdom and prey perches on Jason's wrist.
The artist's eye as if painted on the bird's head stares out
to signify attentiveness. Jason, under an eclipsed sun

around which revolve two planets. Jason, admired
and in love. Always, the artist's eye swerves toward
nourishment. The artist's eye is looking out at us.

FRAME FOR THE FUTURE

A chorus of lovely maidens sings to quiet the waves
to harmonize with the gods that bless such voyages.

Medea has slain artifice, must slay her children.
Jason, self-absorbed, sends off the bird

who will seek ship's passage through the rocks.
Song continues. Two panels to make us compare.

Three to arouse uncertainty. *Argo*: hull, mast, spar.
The canvas is its sail...

Mother Asleep

after a painting by Leon Kossoff

What if the mother
        is always sick,
what if for her whole life,
        she is sick

—when we were children—
        weren't we
always asking: is that sleep
        she is sleeping

or is it a slide toward death?
        What is it
to be always in fear,
        isn't that ridiculous,

that one's hug
        or one's moving too near
could hurt?
        Isn't that *hurtful*?

Don't these thoughts
        pend on a life
like a painter's heavy impasto?
        Don't they distort

what he paints,
        bending it from one
understandable realm
        into the fearful next?

Seeing her in the chair,
        her head atilt,
or lying on her bed,
        the child's eye

inevitably trailed
        away from her being there,
followed the lines
        formed by the drapery of sheets

or by the downward flow
        of hidden limbs,
—gravity pulled at the eye
        and fated it.

And isn't this why
        Kossoff painted
a bright red blotch
        just below his mother's left hand

—nothing structural
        in its being there
—nothing in the image
        or design to fix it,

—red blot
        of a child's anger—
formless,
        homeless—

didn't it wander
        like a loose speck,
like an errant cyst
        in a teary eye?

Within the Open Landscapes

words for the etchings of Jane Joseph

1

Doesn't the picture say
no room in this world for anything more?
If you desire to add something,
you must begin again
and make your own world,
including what has been missing
from the very beginning
of the world.

You must make an enormous effort
to leave this world for that one,
something like dying, if not quite.

Each world is so complete,
terror and emptiness
accompany every effort to leave it.

2

Black parts of things
keep the eye centered on the dark.
At least one can see
a bit of upstanding twig
leads to the branch,
leads along the branch
until the branch
foregrounded before flowing water

invites a sojourn past woods and house
along its banks.

Clouds are always on the move,
and suggest the weather's alterations.
Darks do no more than keep the eye
centered on the dark.

3

When the things of the world
are so carefully depicted
—when we see such things—
surely, we surrender a little, giving
ourselves over to the thing seen.

I have heard others speaking
of the tree's *treeness*
or an object's *being*.
I have looked,
and each time I experience something
—my own disappearance,
my own failed going-out
to meet the tree,
to meet the object.

Nothing coming back.

4

I can love a picture
but only if it doesn't love me.

I insist on boundaries.
I can hate a picture
without it hating me.
I don't insist on boundaries.

5

The branch of the sycamore
forks two ways,
one limb sort of down
and flat across the paper,
the other making an upthrust
so powerful it begins
to curve back on itself
as though the light was the light
of a nourishing self-regard
and the wide-spaced faint scribble
marks that go near the vertical
were the accidental pleas of space itself
warning against hubris.

6

So many bridges, foot, railway, auto,
each obscured by the surrounding designs,
are mythologies of difficult contact.
Or children's stories where ogres
are secreted in dark patches under pathways
by which we connect.

7

The daffodil hangs its heavy-blossomed head.
Wordsworth has shamed you.
And Eliot made the hyacinth
the flower of rebirth
into death's blossoming

You are lone upon the heath.
You are between realms,
between cliché and astonishment.

8

And let the picture transform you.
Let this thistle put on its fiery fall color,
and let its bunched tufts
resemble a wrathful deity,
and let the corolla be a necklace
of enlaced skulls, and let homage be paid
by the ground underfoot,
its otherness crushing
ego's unreasonable hectorings,
and let the mind never rest
in the false nirvana of vegetative happiness,
and let the bumble alight,
thick-dusted with the pollen of awareness.

This Constellation Is a Name (2012)

Maazel Conducts "Arirang," in Pyongyang
(26 February 2008)

> *if you leave me, your feet will be caught*
> *in the mountain passes* —from *Arirang*

If you remain separated from me, your dreams will be
blocked as though by snow in mountain passes.

If we are apart, our dreams will shred on mountain crags,
while beneath them, the passes lie open.

If the snow in passes has melted, freshets of water will run
down both sides of the mountain.

If the flow of the brook begins because of a thaw, we can
say winter lasted just enough, and we need no more.

If the wind makes music in the icy branches of trees, what
sort of music does it make if hard wood clacks against
wood?

If after all this cold, the wind is heard amidst bunched
leaves, will it be the music of the past, the future or for
just now while I hold my hand in yours?

If we hear the same note, will it be like walking in the
light of the one moon though we are in different places?

If the moon shines between clouds, won't the icy paths
gleam as we imagined in the storybooks, unearthly but
bidding?

If we take the paths up through the passes, will we come
   upon figures descending toward us, some with arms
   outstretched?

If your feet are cold, come, at least warm them in the hut
   that sits astride the ridgeline that divides our two places.

After Baudelaire's Le Gouffre

He knew the syllogism
        could not explain
why one day
        slammed into the next,

or why it hurt
        as much to be alive
as knowing something
        bad awaits you.

Why awls of doubt
        painfully nicked
a groove in thought,
        why hopes deceived.

The syllogism
        could not explain
those green islands of desire
        that lie deep inside.

No lines of verse
        in the logic's rationale
to carry him off, nothing there
        to puff out ego's billowed sail.

The syllogism paid no attention
        to all the half-heard talk,
to the nonsense of spun-out thought
        that only entertained.

Thus was the abyss
            carried within,
setting my hair on end,
            while winds of fear passed frequently.

It hurt as much
            to be alive
as knowing something bad
            awaits you.

He gave over night
            to Morpheus,
to seductive figures that startled
            and made sleep suspect.

Dream and nightmare insisted:
            death really
wasn't good enough for us.
            He wasn't sure:

were we mortal or immortal?
            That's why it hurt
so much to be alive,
            knowing something bad
awaits you.

Afikomens

for Harvey Shapiro

NEW YORK CITY

Later, when we gave up talking about ruins,
about the demons who made them
and the contributory demons in ourselves,
I felt a need to note how much I missed
what I had barely made an effort to see.

How one day, some months after the event,
and with no heed to what might be there
in the eye's corner, I crossed Sixth Avenue,
head turned downtown. I was looking south
to where the towers had been. And suddenly,
all that unblocked sky was a reminder to me.
                                        Images
flooded back as though I were looking through
a kind of window between buildings, a window
between souls, an opening that might lead me
to the Jewish god, or at least to that place
where one could imagine His presence,
where one might even place the prohibited idol
or graven image, something to bump up against,
to bow down to, to fill the space.

BEYOND ZERO

According to Rosenzweig,
God has removed himself
to the point of nothingness.
And according to me, mankind,

has been removing itself as well,
unsure of its mode, unsure of its path—
back to the trilobite or fated to remake the planet
in the image of a grand, blinding supernova.

But I do know the one I love in the singular
has taken on an existence beyond the point
of any *somethingness*, more like the taste
before an aftertaste. I'm at least one step removed
from that removed God. How to explain it?
When I move my arm out to hold her hand
or to touch her on the shoulder,
she has already moved with me.

HYPONATREMIA

The nurse said, there's no end of depth to plain water, mean-
ing that water was, chemically, *bottomless*, that there were
no salts to cling to, to exchange—and so, with each sip, one
slipped deeper into its pure blue-white abyss, until a seizure
occurred, and the body shook for a few moments as though
in a wild propitiatory dance that signaled surrender or the
invoking of the void. It was the body then, the body curled
up like a fetus guarding the very last of its sodium, its potas-
sium, those elements, as marked in the periodic table, those
bonds that chain us to the universe.

HUNGARY

The monuments to the warriors rise
above the profiles of the Buda hills.
They punch a hole in the sky, whether

seen from Pest or from the Bridge of Chains.
At night, a spotlight shines on a glittering
bronze sword or a helmet carved of stone.
The light punches a hole in the darkness
over Hungary. In the National Museum,
the next-to-last room is devoted
to the Holocaust and the Nazis.
A dull lamp illuminates the dusty exhibits,
as though a diaphanous, obscuring cloth
were thrown over its glass cases
with their atrocious artifacts, matte black
as the night of time itself, sucking up
the otherwise bright light of a national history.

MON COEUR MIS À NU

I was born in Brooklyn, lived on Pulaski
between DeKalb and Throop.
Odd place to learn about Baudelaire's
three great types: warrior, poet and saint.
But my father was in the National Guard
and in 1943 marched up our block in khakis,
a thin black holster belt across his chest.
He was packing a .45. And at night, playing cards
with his buddies, he'd call up the corner deli
for a dozen pastrami sandwiches, sours and the
    works,
moaning into the phone *how sick he was, how all
    alone he was—*
his friends tittering in the background—could
    someone *please*
deliver the food to the house? To my mother, he
    was a savior,

a saint, throwing away a fortune to help her through her
heart trouble,
to keep her safe. And to my grandfather, Rabbi Zalman
Heller,
his son was a dime-a-dozen bum, an apostate, running
away to sea
when he was only fifteen. Later, he made movies in south
Florida.
The production company went bust fast, as did his real
estate agency.
He wrote poetry.

SHARING

There's nothing like sharing Jewish history in Paris.
The plaques of the dead are everywhere,
and the plaques about the hundreds of *élèves*
taken to the camps are affixed to the wall
of every school where history is shared.

Each part of the story, false or true,
pulls on one, as one tears off a nubbin
from a baguette, each bite hurts
and affects the whole, each morsel
is dry enough to make one choke
as though choking on the whole.

There's nothing like sharing Jewish history in New York.
It's like snapping apart a square of matzoh
or taking a hammer to a pane of glass. Where
one has shared history in New York, there are
only shards and splinters, bits of matzoh *farfel*
to mark the spot. Always the pavement lies

underfoot, always, while the heel grinds
the rest to dust, one has in one's hand
the piece entire.

NATIONAL GEOGRAPHIC

The poems in so many books
are like the barnacles I've seen
in photos of whales, studding
its head and carcass like an old man's
warts and liver spots. There'll
come a time when after I've read
another poem, taken another sounding
of the word's depths, all that reading
will weigh me down, mess up
the relation of my flesh to its ballast.
I won't be able to rise very far
from someone else's deeps.
The sun in the blue sky will shine
like a little disk of poetry
way up there above the surface.

HISTORY

Among the "dirty Jews" of the past, none were as dirty
as those from Poland's shtetls whom the Nazis
and the next-door neighbors fell upon with unprecedented
    fury.
It was no different for the snobbish German Jews
and for the unlucky Sephardim who carried,
like kindling, their utter misplacement, their proud
badge of dignity, into the century's fires.

AT MY FATHER'S GRAVE

This pebble I put on your gravestone
is not to weigh you down
but to bring you up. This pebble
found at the curbside of the cemetery road,
the road that leads to the office where a record
of your interment is kept. This pebble
will mark that your body has gone back
to mingle with earth and with rock,
gone back to what is inert. This little stone,
which can only be itself. I part with this pebble,
as you have parted with what you were
in this world of stones and of bodies.
This pebble is a weight upon a stone,
a weight upon a weight, a presence
upon an absence. I do not part
with my love for you. It is never apart.

Ode to the Sky on the Esplanade of the New

from Tibet: A Sequence

DOUBT

Familiar spirit! If nevertheless this is what you wish to be,

a high sovereign, sky lord of the lit temple,

one who has spoken, embracing the bowl reversed in air,

the majesty of blue, of jade and of iron,

truly, if you are a construct of that which you proclaim:

being, light of all and everything, and one who rises up to and yet

remains fixed under the roof of the great void, surrounded like a wall

of spiraling ether, profoundly hard and pure—

still what deprivation! What prostration of the orb's height

where my forehead reigns at the resting place of the sages,

over the trebled paving that rounds out their image.

What humility belittling my face.

What nakedness raises me toward yours?

What unreasonableness growls as though infused with
    lightning

from the lowest places where, sifting among the self's
    particles,

I am the mere pivot of the millstone that grinds.

RESOLUTION

Is it necessarily thus, beingless one, that you could be

not undeceived? Not yourself, the canceling dust collector.

Not the disappearing. Not transparent. No aim?

Not always, confoundingly, the lone one of your self-vows?

Without doubt and without end, evoking your certitude,

feigning knowledge, I strike three times at my own demons.

I laugh at respect. I glare feverishly toward those at bay.

I strongly sound out hope and distress.

Without fear, heart exposed, flooded by light and water,

I raise with two hands my appeal. I reach out to touch.

Manifestly, it is necessary that you appear to me:

Your sky is not futilely distant, nor your clarity.

See: I await you: I keep the dance to myself,

carrying my spirit, calling for you in the world,

throwing my weight in reverse so that I probe—

a diver plunging toward vertiginous depths under the
ice cap.

CONTEMPLATION

You are, *all at once*, all that you are.

Your true essence and your numerous assumptions,

your names, your attributes: a world your world overwhelms.

Contemplation transformed into rapture.

You are the lord of science, a body more light than smoke,

thus penetrant, burnished until you are pure spirit and its
echoes.

You are rich in years, first one, born from chaos.

You know how to discern the imbecile from the hero.

Glacial, Comforter, Divined Diviner.

One. Exorbitant. Contemplated. Contemplator.

In all that is animate, in which all returns and dies.

Heard. Numerous. Perfume, music and color.

Double. Dome and God. Temple formed of the vault.

Triple. Hundredfold place of the ten thousand ways.

Worried father of all who are bewitched,

your perfect eye profoundly hard and beautiful.

AROUSAL

So beautiful, so perfect in opposition to the human

that I am silenced—my words nulled,

never attaining to the ninth sphere

nor to the space below nor to the spirit lords who have
    fled.

Most high, let us walk the ordered esplanade!

Let us carry high the numerous and the just whirlwinds.

Let us grasp the circle: let us catch the assailing blue.

So high? Without hope: there are no rays.

To aid here: the new embers of our appearance.

Here the three mountains and the renewing of the hours.

Recommencing: strong interior life.

So we must let them blaze! Let us devour flesh and blood.

It is necessary to arouse one's self, its fire crackling, to
burn red.

To penetrate one's heart with the deepest of gouges.

To traverse on the vertical fires that the sky stirs,

carrying ourselves to the level of the horizon filled with
winds.

ECSTASY

Am I really here? Am I, an upstart, so high?

Great peace and name and splendor before and after,

touching the chaos where the sky no longer hopes,

closing itself and flickering like a round eyelid.

Like a drowned one flowing toward the other surface,

my brow newborn in fashion on the horizons

I penetrate and see. I take part with reasons.

I hold the empyrean, and I have the sky for mansions.

I enjoy to the brim, all my spirits. I provoke

my widened awareness to all the senses so quickly

that the spirit is like air. I overflow without limits.

I spread my two arms. I reach almost all the way.

MEDIATION

Here the self's ransom and the crude mediation;

here falls the torrents of rain and of gratitudes,

the sky spilling tears on the fullness of me.

All abundance, a cataract pummeling me.

Dizziness weighs down the flesh and the earth's blood.

Futility of flight so high without lure:

vulture frozen in the blue: agony without death.

To cut the links? Not even a giant dares.

And then all disposes itself and then all is closed and
gloomy.

The yellow taken back. I am to kneel down. To flatten.

On my face, the master's eyes, the eyes living but without
brilliance,

the spirit exhausted, the heart too breathless to beat.

Truly, he has been what was—

Sovereign, lord of sky and temple clear

who has spoken—the bowl reversed in air.

This of your majesty, of blue, of jade and of iron.

The Form

from Tibet: A Sequence
in memory of Armand Schwerner

Has a man sculpted this effort, has a minor god-being
    sketched these bodies,

            innumerable and shapeless, expressionless,
                cryptic, self-secret?

Are they all cut, polished, restored to their stature? Do
    they radiate

            an overflowing confidence, do they embody the
                fullness of themselves?

The good potters of Being who do the turning, turn their
    happy gods like clay pots.

            Are they children when it comes to mankind,
                their muddy hands errant?

Does the base earth flow without laughter; is the form
    ultimately a masque to be quenched

            in tears and under the eye of some spiritual
                henchman repeating the same mistaken form?

Flippant artisans who dare no more than to re-create the
    bon vivant, the cosmopolitan

            —their workings, Tibet, are not like yours.

For you, Tibet, your kneadings are raised to the great
   self-contained strength of yourself:

> you create the molded hero, struck down and
>   touching,

no mere potter but a poet, no maker of art but of poems.

> Tibet, not from outside but from within.

Severe statutory deity, emergent chisel and fire and
   glowing rock,

> you strike your planetary medallion.

Your great proper work, devising your scaled motto:

> "Mountains, sculpture of the earth."

◆

So these villagers have risen into their petty joys, into
   their besotted adventuring—

> dividing space as they march forth into the day,

heads high, inserted flippantly into the furrows of the
   clouds.

> They move as one determined mass, dragging me
>   along, toward the sacred mountain, Omi.

They wear beautiful clothes bedecked with the flowers of
dead azaleas.

What a grand party as they go.

They are decorated like beasts, perfumed with attar of
mystery and transgressed boundaries.

I see their glib preoccupations; they are smooth
talkers, nimble and lighthearted.

Men, garbed in red, women in turquoise. Lithesome, they
carry themselves like captured lords,

their torsos curved, graceful; their faces courteous,
but of a sovereign vagabondage.

O young women, each arrayed like an armored falconress,
arrested in flight,

exhausted yet ever hoping for release.

O young men, gazelles of the blue harness! It is necessary
to see the spirit

neither in rut nor in similar mystical embrace,
neither flirt nor imploring streetwalker.

Enough to be like one who has received a glancing blow to
the shoulder of his spirit.

Enough to climb toward truth from this grandiose
sensual, flexibility.

♦

Suddenly, in the blur of gray fog, in confusion and shame, terrifying and sordid,

I invoke your immense ornamentation, bright unearthed metals

and stones gathered from the mountainsides, fashioned into armor.

The endlessly circling garuda, bird of time and death,

breastplate of silver, cap adorned with jewels, mantle well-made.

Tibet is an encased goddess. Foolishly, I judge you harshly, o teacher,

mocking you like some merchant from Ladak, then drooling over your goodness.

But, at heart, I am more miserable than you. So, in shame, I grasp your being,

your mountains, precious stones, lakes and rocks. I, who hope never to fail henceforth,

who have barely the power to think of you, to pronounce your name, "Tibet!"

Help me, my own ears are still stoppered, my ear hearing
only the inner gossip of a grasping self.

So far, the consequence of precious words seem
small and base.

Tibet, do not efface me nor leave me too humiliated.

My name comes back to me as in a glance from
the book of ciphers.

Dianoia (2016)

Mappah

This brocaded cloth is nothing in itself, neither real nor unreal, woven with an edge that is no edge.

No one can safely say where the sacred leaves off, where the profane begins.

The teacher remarked that to regard the earth as the shrine-room floor is enlightenment.

The sheath was slipped from the Torah to reveal the scrolls, the Torah laid upon its stand, the scrolls were opened for the day's reading.

Some believe a god keeps the process going. Others, that if there is just one god or many, they can want nothing of us, else how could they be gods?

I'm not sure of a god's existence, even as I shy away from those who insist they keep company with one.

But if a god wants the person's marrow, as with Job, then the visible and invisible ways by which a god manifests are extensions of a hunger.

Which is why such weight is given to the delusions that make us happy. Is it madness to kneel before the sea, to say a prayer over something like a piece of hard candy?

Yet everything that is the case continues, and I am left with a suspicious sorrow that we grieve neither for truth nor falsity.

Someone lifts and folds the cloth, someone follows the Hebrew with the *yod*, the sculpted finger cast in gold. *Davar* and *davar*.

Signs of revelation are shown forth, the dulled angel of history, our brighter angel of catastrophe.

Let this be put another way: the cloth that shielded the Torah from light shielded light from the Torah.

Remember in historic Paris, the pause before the *mappah* in its glass case, the embroidery, the traceries of dedication to the patron's daughter, lamé and beadwork?

Remember the heartbreak, the cry *to wake the dead and restore what has been lost*?

During periods of calm, an adequate vocabulary was found among cynics.

But introduce a little danger or show people running for their lives, and how quickly attention focused on words like *bread* or *child*.

One thought in afterthoughts, of the saved, of the living. *So it went on.*

After disaster or terror, each declension in the name of a god became fixed.

In the fires, the weavings burned with the parchment.

Smoke rises, blackens.

Let this be put another way: the cloth that wrapped the Torah in darkness shielded the light from the dark.

Let this be put another way, let this be put differently, the wish to call out.

Abide with Me a Moment

*meditating on the writing of
Allen Grossman (1932–2014)*

Just to say—*sun rising and setting*,
that poignancy of the world machine—

I was reading you, your "how to do things
with tears," a friend eulogizing

with the words "how we wept," and I asked
myself, perhaps you asked, were there tears

on the face of the "mystical godhead," that
edifice as implacable as edifices are?

Scholem—this is a "Jewish" poem alright—
his book tells of Ezekiel's divine throne,

substance there amid time's myriad shadows,
yet before time. And I guess if one can call it

a belief, then mine was, if nothing else,
the Holy One had gone missing, and I was left

to raise other thrones from the now abandoned
languages of observation and objection.

And here was the twist, that if we conceived
the Holy One manifests only as speech,

when for me the words "Holy One" were a
locution for what is nameless, for the "*I am*

that I am" (did He read Descartes too?)
with no residue and no hope, who was

to cast a canonical light so that
we might not stumble or fall on the path

that led through the biblical grasses? Please abide,
because I, to you Allen Grossman, am trying

to ask how your words sought a place in the
argument that bends one from the non-Jew

to the Jew, the way the *Shoah* turns all
who know of it into the Jew or the non-Jew,

as if the old story of the "Holy One"
were now the new one about language,

as if we sought too far back for a
tabula rasa on which Paradise and Eden

were inscribed, so that a poetry of tears
would still leave a portion of the earth

in worshipful form, the sacred as
insurance against unwarrantable flight.

Dianoia

Years are given to the poem's cut,
you say *language*, you say hardest

of earths, each word a narrowing,
less light, *lightless*, a blind pursuit.

Objects and flesh make one feel better.
Pain, bother—mind as sharp testimony,

but it feels like a plow in stony ground,
rutting in a self, shattering your last words,

breaking apart clods of what was named.
You are saying be subversive, you

are not saying time or water
will humble the rock, for now

old ways must yield, the groove
you made is without exit, and just

as you were born you will die
with belief anyway...

Notes on Notes

Had hoped for Buddhas: *the wrathful deities beringed*
in flames and adorned with the skulls of others, their
    clawed
feet standing on the ego's neck, on the root of the soul, the
    heart,

and the human. They are real one told oneself *they will*
    slit
the throats of those who pretend to own their selfhood
or their perceptions. They always take the side of the
    cosmos.

So why the bleak view? Don't you live among the
    ordinary,
between the ability to exist and the premonition that one
    doesn't,
between red brick and a zip code, between *thereness* and
    location?

Maybe you over-rely on science: TV ads or bad movies
    talked away,
no more than the sky's rain of microparticles passing
    painlessly
through the body. The guns, the war crimes, the.... Yes,
    terror and

dread are a portion, as prayers for the day and the homily
    are a portion.
Whose turn to gather up Antigone as she gathered her
    brother's remains?

Whose turn to be Phocion's wife in Poussin's painting,
bringing home

her husband's ashes? Some days I cannot use the third
person "he," can
barely indulge the "you" of the wish-fulfilling witness.
I've fallen in
with the spirit of the "I," the "I" that lost credibility, that
indeterminate "I"

soon to become a "who" as in "who died?" I have tried to
be a narrator.
OK, I'm also the mysterious traveler waking beside a
mountain or sitting
by a river, back to a city, fed by busyness and fear, *not
feeling like myself.*

How soiled and tattered the shred-ends of the published
counselors,
their papered slogans: *never mind, you live; never mind,
you are.*
There's always a honeyed sun, if not shining, at least to
remember.

There is always a body, a memory. Words may be trite or
stained
by commerce but also consoling. My text has brought me
together
with my longing. I've been promised, on the edge of the
indefinable,

an apparitional beauty, an e*rscheinung*, to surround me
like amber

around a fly. O this aura, O companion to the days ahead, days filled with
biblical sweetness, a rebuke to those who hoped for an alternative paradise.

There

There are those for whom figures
on balconies exist, if only as possibilities.

People in photographs with arms
outstretched in salute or worship

before the empty terrace where
a figure is meant to appear—for now,

for repeated scenes, for always.

And there are those with their politics, their
fears and hopes caught in those adoring thrusts,

who must make their gestures even as they
are the ones whose gestures will be mocked

even as that mocking is accounted for.

There exists the brushed-back reticence of the "I"
that makes one otherworldly to the world, *un autre*,

as in Rimbaud's case, enslaved, the poet wrote,
by his baptismal rite. So it is with ritual, with repeats

of word or act—the forms insist on want, on warmth
desired as at a drafty window. It is all clear, clear

as that sun-filled winter day, lucent, brutal
and severe, with so much glare the scene

seems pathless, static in its brilliance.

Internet Enabled

Turns out, Tirso de Molina, 16th-century Spanish monk,
born of *conversos*, dreamed up top trickster Don Juan.

150 years later, Emmanuele Conegliano, converted Jew,
a.k.a. Lorenzo da Ponte, penned the libretto for *Don
  Giovanni*.

Online journal *Tablet Magazine* claims these origins,
  despite
the Catholic faith of all characters and composer as well,

make this, perhaps Mozart's greatest work, "a Jewish
  opera."
Turns out, according to the Internet, Don Giovanni's ethos
  runs

an electronic river through paranoid URL after URL:
no one truly good can do much to save anyone from evil,

not even a loving Christ, whose open arms and forgiveness
are as naught to a sociopath like Don Giovanni, so best to
  kill,

and if needed get what you need to get according to the
  Internet
with its hate sites, ads for AK-47s, designs for IEDs, for gas
  attacks.

But let's surf back to Mozart. His opera, beautiful, so
  lovely in fact

Yiddish poet Glatshteyn writes, instead of God, we should revere

Mozart, whose music surpasses in holiness the Sermon on
    the Mount.
I agree. Despite my irreligion, I have a deep love for *Don
    Giovanni*'s

divine last chorus, the one directors often cut, in which
    singers sing
of justice triumphant over evil after the villain has been
    led to the pit.

If the Abrahamic god exists, he's hidden, never graven, his
    voice
profound in the Commendatore's implacable, graveled
    m'invitasti.

Visit

The descendant kings rule
over rock-strewn littoral, banked clouds,
hyssop hills of Jordan, shimmer that concedes
the intelligible to a sheer impossibility of landscape.

Believe—some god behind the edged shrubs, the pebbles,
the near flat glassiness of sea. Human needs contract,
matter little. Curls of viscous foam at shoreline.
Tour bus inching between wary-eyed soldiers.

Concede they grew from hardened land, clad in khaki.
Tour guide provender reminds: this body of water excludes.
After the mud baths of Ein Gedi—here David took refuge
    from
murderous Saul—conqueror trinkets on sale in the gift
    shop.

Martyrdom of Masada, Herod's palace farther on the road.
Marker "300 feet below sea-level." Around this lowest
    point,
earth mere bowl. Bottom of the world, bottom of language.
Inscriptions in rock, echolalia in the caves of the Scrolls.

Canonical

Seven times a day I praise you for your righteous laws
—Psalm 119

Canonical hours, hours according to law when the world
stops for a pause that sometimes befalls us. Remember,
it was the ancient Jews who made these hours, hours
that are old before Calvary, those oldest matins, lauds and
    terce.
Dante invoked the sacred hours. In *Inferno*, Canto XXXIV
it is mid-terce of Holy Saturday and his "Dante" hangs
    suspended
in the lowest *bolgia* bewildered that his descent has
    brought him
so close to Lucifer's waist. There, at Hell's core, antipodal
to Jerusalem and to his slain and risen Christ, in the place
"where weight bears down from everywhere," he begs
    Virgil
"lighten my darkness."
Lighten my darkness—perhaps what is canonical
happens not in hours but in mere moments, in saintly
    accidental
moments when we swerve into deepest doubt. Today, just
as the Passover began, and seventy years after the event
    itself,
I heard a recording of the just-freed survivors of Bergen-
    Belsen
singing *Hatikvah*. And suddenly, I was outside of what
    exists.
I felt myself reduced to one enormous sob and could no
    longer
imagine my life or life on the planet. The rest of that day,
through its vespers, lauds and complines, my salubrious
    body

was in denial. It had gone into hiding behind itself.
It had fled this deluded world of canonical hours.
It shrank from time, from the unbearable time of that
unbearable singing. The singers sang for the dead,
and what inhabited this body of mine wanted to join them.
The moment had arrived to keep time with those clocks
that kept time in hell and in purgatory. In paradise,
the absent god could not hear those clocks tick.
Nothing that ever existed could time itself to
the beat of that song, that song sung so unbearably.

My Grand Canal

I

This, for the overwritten city,
for the sheen of its domes above waterline
viewed at night from the vaporetto—at least at night,
for the rise in the throat, the longing
always present, but not to be addressed
by the cynic, this, the ache for an ethics of wonder,
thread between numinous threads, now waters,
now burnished light, yet harmonious
before suffering—insufficient, sentimental,
smacking of sentiment at least, with its question of what
is to be repaired, is there something to repair?

II

This for the syllabaries. Wordsworth's
"Once did she hold the gorgeous East in fee,"
O art, eliding a darker history,
city that coined the word "ghetto."
But the gold-lit domes, *oro*, ore, as in shimmer,
as in sweet vocables he "sighed his soul toward,"
sweet uplift out of those histories.
How is one prepared for this?
Hath not a tourist ears? Hath not a tourist eyes?
Betimes, this plinth of desires, its concatenations of
    simulacra.

III

Old Ez, entombed on San Michele,
you can be redeemed,
but outside of time
when the verse will be read as cut
beyond the right and wrong of it.
Can this be allowed, this conciliation
as little miracles are allowed
their utterance?

IV

And there betimes, baroque San Moisè,
Moses and his Law honored, not in horned marble,
but on Meyring's altarpiece, where on Mount Sinai
he receives the Tablets. Old Testament prophets—
their voices interrupt chronology—
their graven images blent into divine illuminations.
Onsweep. *O blind mores*, the Grand Canal flows out
toward that isle of the dead.

V

Benefice in wonder. Almost sunset.
San Marco and its lions dissolve
in briny air, imagined space, imagined sound.
MJQ, Milt Jackson's vibes, Connie Kay's brush on cymbals,
The Golden Striker, to-be-figured sun of *No Sun in Venice*.
Only the dumbstruck find miracle
without context, which is why the notes remind me
that along canal's byways, in the small churches

Titian and Carpaccio deliquesce—
O Western candles—
to be in love with their tapering.
And I am borne by a watery light
that flows us toward the *now*,
only to disappear among the eons,
matter, gravity, holding in the currents
as though we were each an offering.

Fatigue God

from Tibet: A Sequence

Daughter of force, daughter of arduous mountains,
  mistress to this exhausted corpse

  who journeys into fatigue—here, at last, this
    intoxicated hour

when the Hindu chanter and the night distill a pungent
  herb.

  Fluid song, burning, cunning—

yet highest of offerings: god-poison in the bejeweled
  begging bowls.

  I drink the fatigue, my idol, my daemon.

I am shaken by these preparatory rhythms. I incant the
  music, mortar and pestle

  pulverizing instruments of a drunken sacrifice—

the self in its weighted march to quotidian supplications.

  Feet to this rockbound earth, imagined talons

that grip down and crush, and draw upon the earth's
  sapience that invigorates.

  Extract of the human mandrake—

press, grind and gather this gift up into the arms of the
    royal king.

   We are cattle, felled before this sovereignty.

Tremors of the limbs shaken by insatiable devotion.

   The emptiness exquisitely deflates itself.

I consecrate my weariness, my words as slogan, as trophy,
    a sole wish,

      this gift of being, this undiscoverable realm, this
         muteness that wants to speak.

Wrathful Deity Posing as the Physical Object of Desire

from Tibet: A Sequence

I defend myself from love, Tibet, from its vexatious
familiarity.

Still, my hymn of love is reserved for you.

Cursed Tibet, you understand my discreet ardor in being
your lover.

Look here (my amour cannot be more than a tiny
portion of the love you receive)!

You hold divinity to the ends of the earth, godhood as
diverse as your mountains.

Most difficult of demons.

Nevertheless you are near and seem truly to have carried
me into this life.

To live is to be provoked into grand combat.

Yet my own defensiveness encloses; I live in unfulfilled
retreat, unsatisfied.

I am my own obstacle, blocked from the gap in being
where my heart fights.

Between a great love and myself, between us, there is this
amour/armor.

My flesh—unique in spite of you.

In spite of your all-seeing eyes, shielded from my knowing
yet gleaming like points of finery.

I am subdued, but seek to rise from my submission.

I must surmount you unsurrendered—frozen polar realm,
peak of the mountains.

Where is it written I must be vanquished, where is it
written that the climb is endless?

Here naked, white, high—anticipation is already my
satisfaction.

I have won from you, this faceted gleam, this
simulacrum of companionship.

High Basin

from Tibet: A Sequence

To collect myself there in the mountain's cut: to bathe in
the self's pool:

all its stories—of myself, *to* myself—gathered, and led
into runnels,

to flow from on high to low, flux without root or
rootedness,

useless to name, useless except to surrender and admit

the shame of wanting the unknowable, incessantly casting
and retrieving the bait

of the ego, as though before a watershed teeming with life.

The gods must be fond of laughing. Your warriorship
enclosed between

a helmet of sky overhead and the rock's amphitheater,
armor hard from its hollowing,

plaything of the self's interior winds.

But to heal again I turn to your example Tibet, rich with
adventures.

Can I imitate your sacred lake, Yam dok-Tso, outlet to
the West?

Doubled lake—lake—twice set in its liquid nomination, word/thing

of mind, only mind, distilled as though a secondary water.

Can I also, by hyperbole and sequence, journey there?

Transport from level to level,

to move with high compassion and swelling O calculator

to be—to the ninth power, for all beings,

and almost to the centuple fold, to the crescent (growing) number,

without denial.

And also following toward infinity.

New Poems

Back Among Them

Thus, back on the road
as though one never left it.
(I've had my stationary moments.)

Back with a phrase
and I will march on unto a sentence.

Homonyms and assonance,
rhythms and conceits, the paper,

the text, the revealed concealments,
the phase that is being got through.

Someone will note that but for the "r"
there's consonance between phrase and phase,

The mystic will say the dropped "r"
begins righteousness, which is not over, not yet.

The "r" that starts righteousness
has not been lost.

There has been much stationary movement.

But the road is back before one (not before us or me,
    maybe you?
I can't speak for you—not a beckoning as though there
    were a choice).

This is the road. For this wear a monk's sandals,
or like Mandelstam's Dante, acknowledge the tread.

The direction going back, the sorrows that reach from below to heaven.

Tedium. I can speak for myself, I love boredom. It's a long way to go, where will you find it?

The Whole Life

Where to put the whole life?
Can one put it anywhere?

On the page, it can't be looked at,

because there was a war,
and the father already wore khakis,

and there were frigid winters
and mother's hair black as the Hudson.

Then her heart knocked badly.
Could you see the life, the whole life?

◆

Interregnums of night and absence.

One's companions: the radio's green eye,
the animals hidden in sofa cushions' shapes.

The steam pipes knocked in the house;
in the school, the steam fogged glass.

◆

Then came the warm south.

The whole light of Florida, pink buildings,
sun, green, water. Salt cakes the inner life.

Your hopes bleed into adolescence.
Every day, every day. The library,

the young body you dream about.

Everything waits, as if a god
puts off convincing reason and passion.

◆

The return is to a different cold, to the word as connection.
Star utter, quantum utter. Laughter and humiliation.

You are at last home, re-branded, re-buried in the libraries,
in bituminous air. Now the years seem folios of paper,

thicker than reams pierced by memory's spike.
Parents dead, the work re-orphans you,

each word displaces toward dark and light.
About love, you've hardly said anything.

This is an exercise, an exorcism.
You can't look—what is there to see?

You loved the ghosts of pasts not one's own,
the romance with honorable images,

the correct, the courageous, the words
that leak sepia into the present.

Re-Searches

Our grim cruel machines. Read Milton on Euripides
—the tragedian's verse in *Electra* charmed Sparta
to spare Athens, but then there's Milton, his
On the late Massacre . . . asking God to avenge
"Who were thy Sheep and in their antient Fold"
whom the *Piemontese* "roll'd Mother
with Infant down the Rocks." This grimy machine
of poetry, portioning off the *logos* proclaimed divine.
When did poets *not* live in destitute times,
nourished and nuanced on decades of bloody
adventures? *Pull down thy vanity.* IT COHERES,
the works of man in the work of lyric *salve, solvent,*
no key to unlock hidden bliss or faintest hope.
No exemption for that poet who wrote
of the messiah arriving on a tank, or that other
who began each pitch into the doom machine
with a pastoral, urban in its love of sunsets
through bridgeworks, music of jazz and blues,
city scene spiraling from streetscape
to the planes that blew out skylines and littered
plazas with those who jumped from heights
—medieval, a few speared on metal palings
or the trees' forked branches. New strange fruit.
Yet no logic nor words could divide us, plein air,
nor would Cartesian symmetry balance the sharp passions
of our bodies. We sang, we sang our masking music
flowing cleanly through the self; we counter-sang abide
with me, *kol nidre, om* chant, Blake's psalm, all kiddush,
    kid-ish.

Colloquia

I

"World, World," you wrote,
as though martyred to the visible,

the words one chose
would have to say it.

If the famous rosy-fingered dawn
existed, it existed to be proclaimed,

as did the catalog of phrases to embrace,

sheer gorgeousness and vibratory
power of words

to upend those imprisoning
geometries of the conventional.

◆

To articulate mind's paean
imagine the silken net of her,

the sheathed stone of towers
we walked around—

word, words to *world, world*—

reluctantly including the age's
horrors we read about.

Love and desire as possibilities,
as possible suppressions
in a world raped by its ideologies.

Did relief come as compensation
in the words?

What to say for the rock's display of striations
emblazoned above a flowing creek,

the deliberation describing the insect crawl,
its *"chitinous wings,"* that reminded you

of Pound's wasp, and in that moment,
you forgave him his politics
(thus sharpening some issues at hand).

Best, you said, to be "unteachable."

Yet so many lived blindsided by the digital algorithms
of their tribes, arrogant in their insistence and consensus,
the bard's finikins strewn across a wasteland.

Thucydides reminding us, "in evil times, words changed
their common meanings, to take those now given them."

And you said, the problem was failure, no prominence,
only the ditch from which all was seen. *"World, World,"*

I believe you meant something like the cosmos.
"There is something to stand on."

That was as close as one should come to belief.

II

And I remember the teacher's *sadhana* proclaiming:
This world, the trees, the greenery, the Great Wrathful
    One,

you incite, you are the irritant from which
love and hate spring. And I remember

the nights I broke free—eye at the reticle
open to dark skies, charts laid on the table,

dome under dome: "*say I looked at the stars/say*
there was love in the sky/but it wasn't enough."

Youth's dream: to be of that chorus. There it was
and *this in which*, however entrapped,

I gazed at an open starlit field, pristine immensities,
thoughts pliable as the wind swirling around objects

—a little pain, a little bother—one's mind fumbling,
finding only its anguish real. Redemption: an image

on a reflecting mirror...

III

The world is the case (and it is beautiful), thanks LW.

The world is the case, surely the praise poet has a case to
    make.

The world is the case encased.

Seen from outer space.

Ice orbed.

IV

> *—descend so that you may ascend* —Augustine

Trees darkening the ground. Constellations overhead.
Midway, you'd want to go into the subject—then I'd go.

We'd call it prayer if you like.
We'd both desire to walk on, to be happy.

Not much talk but for an occasional comment
on "the compost of history."

And I did make something of a prayer for myself,
I called out: Dante, help me with a fourfold allegory,

one that begins with a beast, a griffon or Sphinx,
and works its way to joyful singing, as in *Purgatorio*,

"*in exitu Isräel de Aegypto*," that "anagogically"
speaks of souls who from the Shoah did not escape

but rose in ashes to somewhere else, sanctified
from corruption by our inability to forget, and I meant,

my dear guide, let's go no farther, but turn at this point
and backtrack along the *bolgias*, for to "go up" is to be
    perfected,

even if to walk past the condemned as they suffer reminds
    them
of their shame. It was by this way, past the limbo of ancient
    poets,

beyond their need to traverse desire, that we would return
to the dark wood from which youth makes its descent,

this time into age. Here, where leaves lay crushed underfoot
and autumn awaited winter, we would emerge into a dark
    expanse,

and name the liminal objects outlined by the stars' dim
    light
as though they were signs of the visionary.

Our Times

from Tibet: A Sequence

I

It is not only the horror and vertigo of power

      which holds this strange land,

Nor is it this austere and superb affront, this roar

      of insolence

Butting its head, its elephantine disregard

      for the rebellious country.

Its lawlessness that echoes in the small valleys.

      It is the unattended flatlands

Surrounded by forests, the foliage strangely familiar.

      The disturbing power that makes

one crazy, wanting to chant to the flowers.

      I knew these valleys

before the madness, its denizens living as though with the

    slow will

of lichens, almost sealed

to the bedrock as though by gods

who want to protect us from the irrational.

High valleys, where sanity and calm reigned, sweetness

as though from the heights, yet something

of their nature

reached down out of high dream, out of the fantasies that

besmirched their hearts

and made of them reliquaries

twisted from the blackest of branches until they shone in

the light.

II

They reconcile themselves...they approach...they bring

themselves to it,

walkers well-stocked with words.

This herd makes for a well-traveled route, these hagglers

with neither fear nor laziness,

as they find entrances into their deepest selves on their

way

to the trading posts.

They make the clocks sound Time, their silly ticking

mechanisms.

They arrive: they dissolve. Even the shade of the camel

palms celebrates their coming with

rustling noise.

This is all, this is *also* following *also*.

I'm here too, at the edge of space, reclusive and silent,

the beggar of the infinite,

neither restless nor shy while all are imploring, chanting a

hymn about the restlessness of their travels.

La La, their singing in their tents echoes off the walls:

"I am not the author of myself, but I am in my domain,

my emptiness."

So passes this grand caravan!

Nothing to mount, nothing to descend to, just one age

passing into another.

There lies the glacier, the ice-steps mounting above the

trade routes, but they fear. This is their sovereignty.

They slide and hurtle past the moraine. *Du temps.*

III

There the same height, here too this level, I search

frantically for the Other (I repeat myself), *je cherche*

l'Autre!

The queen of this kingdom of somewhere else awaits

while I run disheveled toward a paradise with no

apostle.

The Other imagines itself, immense, blocking the way

to desire.

Diverted, the game of love made a mockery. And you ask

whose being is here for you, what

weathers of the mind, what phantoms?

Love bites with its beautiful mouth.

And you hear the sounds of the high spirits reigning,

and you are reduced to silence as you approach

and inhale the scent of love, sweet on the skin. Beware

the Other, the sickly blanched

equivocator, the decoy that the mind constructs.

In these high realms the air is thin, philosophy is the

moving skein

of cloud-work. Be wary.

This is the festival. Silence and joy.

Notes to the Poems

The poems in this collection are presented in rough chronological order. Volume titles are in bold capital letters, with poem titles in small caps.

A LOOK AT THE DOOR WITH THE HINGES OFF (2006)

These poems are from the 1960s, many written in the Spanish seaside village of Nerja from September 1965 to October 1966, and are dedicated to two close friends and early influences: the late Ernie Raia (1937–2006) and the poet Hugh Seidman (b. 1940), both students of Louis Zukofsky at Brooklyn Polytechnic.

OK EVERYBODY, LET'S DO THE MONDRIAN STOMP

This poem is based on *Composition in Red, Blue, and Yellow* by the Dutch painter Piet Mondrian (1872–1944).

EARTH AND CAVE (2006)

This mixed-genre work of poetry and prose was begun in 1966 in Nerja and completed in New York City during the first months after returning from Spain.

WHITE PLUMED REEDS

"Yerba buena" refers to the particular local species of mint, which varies from region to region in Spain.

ACCIDENTAL CENTER (1972)

This was the first full-length collection of my poems.

PRESSURE:
Novi refers to the *Novi Vinadolski*, a Yugolinia passenger-carrying freighter that, in the 1960s, plied the Atlantic from Brooklyn's Erie Basin to Morocco and the Mediterranean.

KNOWLEDGE (1979)

BIALYSTOK STANZAS
Bialystok, in Poland, is where the Heller family comes from. Much of Bialystok's history, including the Polish community in New York and the destruction of its Jewish population by the Nazis in World War II, is contained in David Sohn's *Bialystok: Photo Album of a Renowned City and Its Jews the World Over* (1951), the basis for much of this sequence. In section 9 (Coda) of the poem, *dy-yanu* (also spelled *dayenu*) is from the Passover Seder song and means: "it would have sufficed."

AFTER MONTALE
Eugenio Montale (1896–1981) was an Italian poet who won the 1975 Nobel Prize in Literature.

AT ALBERT'S LANDING
Albert's Landing is a public beach and park between Springs and Amagansett on the east end of Long Island. *"The naked very thing"* is from "Childe Roland to the Dark Tower Came" by Robert Browning.

SPECULUM MORTIS
The title translates as "death's mirror." See Philippe Ariès's *The Hour of Our Death* (1951).

INTERMINGLINGS
"Marks of weakness, marks of woe" is a line from William Blake's

poem "London." "Westcliffe" is a small mountain town in Colorado, under the Sangre de Cristo range.

STANZAS ON MOUNT ELBERT
Mount Elbert is the highest mountain peak (14,440 feet) in Colorado. *Wanderer in the Clouds* is the title of a painting by the German painter Caspar David Friedrich (1774–1840).

IN THE BUILDED PLACE (1989)

WITH A TELESCOPE IN THE SANGRE DE CRISTOS
The Sangre de Cristo mountain range runs from southern Colorado into New Mexico.

FATHER PARMENIDES
Parmenides of Elea was a fifth-century BC philosopher, whose metaphysical and paradoxical writings greatly influenced later philosophical thinkers, hence the "Father" often attached to his name.

MOON STUDY
"O bright!/O bright!" is from the Japanese poet Myōe (1172–1232), often called "the poet of the moon." The haiku is famous for having been written with only one character: "bright."

IN THE BUILDED PLACE
The epigraph is from William Blake's poem "London." "Consciousness in concentric whorls" is taken from the writings of Pierre Teilhard de Chardin (1881–1955).

PHOTOGRAPH OF A MAN HOLDING HIS PENIS
The poem is based on an image by the artist and photographer Michael Martone (b. 1941), not to be confused with the fiction writer of the same name.

SESTINA: OFF-SEASON
A realibus ad realiora is Latin for "from reality to the most real," from Saint Augustine.

ON A LINE FROM BAUDELAIRE
"The dead, the poor dead, have their bad hours" is a translation by Robert Lowell of Baudelaire's *"Les morts, les pauvres morts, ont de grandes douleurs"* in "La servante au grand coeur dont vous étiez jalouse."

SOME ANTHROPOLOGY
The idea for this poem came from a letter in *The New York Times* on January 8, 1988, signed by a group of anthropologists under the title "The Gentle Tasaday Are Merely a Persistent Hoax," a response to an article in the *Times* on May 13, 1986, entitled "The Tasaday Revisited: A Hoax or Social Change at Work?"

IN A DARK TIME, ON HIS GRANDFATHER
"The just man and the righteous way / wither in the ground": Zalman Heller was said to have written a Talmudic study in German, which translates into English as *The Just Man and the Righteous Way*.

FOR UNCLE NAT
"The necessary ten": To open the ark and begin services in a synagogue, ten males over the age of thirteen—the minyan, as it is called—must be present. This poem was written to celebrate my uncle Nathan Heller's eightieth birthday.

ACCIDENTAL MEETING WITH AN ISRAELI POET
The Israeli poet is the late Yehuda Amichai (1924–2000) who taught at New York University in the 1980s.

PALESTINE
"Baudelaire / watched the Negress in the street stomp her feet / and imagine date palms." This image is taken from Baudelaire's poem "Le Cygne."

MAMALOSHON

The title is Yiddish for "mother's tongue" or "native language."

WATER, HEADS, HAMPTONS

"To the white sands who will speak a name?" is derived from Hart Crane's line "To the white sand I may speak a name, fertile" in "O Carib Isle."

IN THE MOUNTAINS, LINES OF CHINESE POETRY:

The epigraph is from "Wanderer's Song" by Meng Chiao, translated by A. C. Graham in *Poems of the Late T'ang.*

WORDFLOW (1997)

LECTURE WITH CELAN

The italicized text is from *Paul Celan: Collected Prose,* translated by Rosmarie Waldrop (1986).

STANZAS AT MARESFIELD GARDENS

The museum contains a replica of Freud's consulting room and houses many of the antiquities he collected. *Adamah* is Hebrew for "ground" or "earth" and is related to the name of Adam in the Old Testament.

IN PARIS

In 1996, terrorists set off bombs in the RER station under Boulevard St. Michel and on the Champs-Élysée. Goldenberg's restaurant was attacked by terrorists in 1982.

EXIGENT FUTURES (2003)

CYCLICAL

The epigraph is from Divani Shamsi Tabriz (thirteenth-century Persian), the son of an Imam and friend and sometimes mentor of Rumi (1207–1273).

"WE CAN ONLY WISH *VALEAT QUANTUM VALERE POTEST.*"
The Latin proverb *"valeat quantum valere potest"* can be translated as "let it be valued according to its power." The italicized text is from a Sumero-Akkadian glossary.

WINTER NOTES, EAST END
Bardos in Tibetan Buddhism is the intermediate states, lasting forty-nine days, between death and reemergence into another life. "It is not possible to contract for a stay" is a line from Armand Schwerner's poem "The Work."

ESCHATON (2009)

ON A PHRASE OF MILOSZ'S
Czeslaw Milosz (1911–2004) was a Polish poet and writer who won the 1980 Nobel Prize in literature. "Rilke's panther" refers to "The Panther" by Rilke. In Cid Corman's translation of the poem, the panther's gaze from his cage, enters the body and "stops being in the heart."

MY CITY
This poem was written after the attacks of September 11, 2001. "The hole in the downtown / sky" refers to the very visible gap left in the New York skyline by the fall of the World Trade Center.

BANDELETTE DE TORAH
The *Yod* is used by the rabbi to point to the words being read as he intones from the Torah. *Davar* is Hebrew for both "word" and "thing." *Aleph*, the first letter of the Hebrew alphabet, is believed by kabbalists to be the primary instance of language, revelatory of all words and hence of all creation.

FOUR LONDON WINDOWS
The section entitled "Westminster" was written after a visit to Westminster Cathedral that happened to coincide with the anni-

versary of the death of T. S. Eliot. William Blake's text can be found in *The Poetry and Prose of William Blake* edited by David Erdman.

HOMAN'S ETCHINGS
Jan Homan (1919–1991) was a Dutch painter and etcher. *Anemos* and *bosanemoon* are Dutch for "anemones," and *tak esdoorn* is Dutch for maple branch.

REPORT ON THE DISPATCHES
Throughout Operation Desert Storm, military briefings of the press were to news accuracy—to borrow from Talleyrand—what military music is to music. Many terms (one thinks of "surgical strike" or "pinpoint bombing") had lost semantic significance as they were employed in massaging the psyches of reporters and, therefore, of readers.

THE ASSUMPTION
Paula Rego (b. 1935) is British painter of Portuguese descent.

IN IRONS
The title is a sailing term that describes the situation when the boat's prow is turned directly into the wind and the sail merely flaps, losing motive force, and the boat makes no headway.

STANZAS WITHOUT OZYMANDIAS
This poem, related to Shelley's "Ozymandias," contains imagery from the landscape of the Great National Sand Dunes Monument in southern Colorado.

ESCHATON
The title comes from the Greek *oschatos/eschate*, meaning to be about last things.

ORDINARINESS OF THE SOUL
The italicized first four lines are from "Along the river" by Lorine Niedecker.

AN INTERPELLATION
"Interpellation" is defined as the formal right of a parliament to submit questions to the government, i.e., to criticize the policies of a governing body, hence, also, an interruption into the way things are done.

THE AGE OF THE POET
Rilke, in a letter to his Polish translator, asks whether one is able any longer to use words like "house," "home," or "tree."

LETTER AND DREAM OF WALTER BENJAMIN
All italicized text is from the writings of Walter Benjamin (1892–1940).

COMMENTARY IS THE CONCEPT OF ORDER FOR THE SPIRITUAL WORLD
The title of the poem is from the writings of Gershom Scholem (1897–1982). The italicized text *he is most apt* is from the writings of Franz Rosenzweig (1886–1929), a philosopher of Judaic thought and culture.

BECKMANN VARIATIONS AND OTHER POEMS (2010)
"Beckmann Variations" is a mixed-genre, prose and poetry meditation focused on the life, paintings, and writings of the German painter Max Beckmann (1884–1950).

INTO THE HEART OF THE REAL
The Sphinxes in Beckmann's painting are modeled on two Sphinxes that sit atop the gate posts of Wertheim Park, which was named for a Jewish philanthropist, in Amsterdam, the city Beckmann fled to on the morning of July 19, 1937, after hearing Hitler's speech the night before praising the Nazi exhibition *Entartete Kunst* ("Degenerate Art"), which was opening that day in Munich. Beckmann by then had been marked as a "degenerate artist," and his work was prominently displayed in the exhibition. In Amsterdam, shortly

after the Nazi occupation, the Dutch collaborationist mayor had the Wertheim name removed from the Sphinx pillars. The German word *Abtransport*, which was the title of Beckmann's painting, is the same word used to designate the deportation of the Jews of Germany and the Netherlands to the death camps.

MOTHER ASLEEP

This poem is based on a painting by the British artist Leon Kossoff (1926–2019).

THIS CONSTELLATION IS A NAME (2012)

AFIKOMENS

The title refers to the *afikomen*, the piece of matzoh broken off during the Passover Seder ceremony and hidden for a child to find and receive a gift. The plural *afikomens* suggests attendance at many Seders, hence a long life. Hyponatremia is a life-threatening condition, often affecting athletes such as marathon runners, where the ingestion of too much water dilutes the body's electrolytes, producing convulsions and coma. *Mon coeur mis à nu* is the title of Baudelaire's prose journal.

ODE TO THE SKY ON THE ESPLANADE OF THE NEW

The poems in this volume designated as from *Tibet: A Sequence* are part of an ongoing project based on Victor Segalen's *Odes suivies de Thibet* (1979). Intermingling his words with mine, these poems are not "translations." As Huan Saussy points out in his introduction to Segalen's *Stèles*, Segalen's poems are "translated from a language that does not anywhere else exist." In *Odes suivies de Thibet*, Segalen takes up his interests in Buddhist and Taoist thought, attempting at times to mimic the language of the sages whose genius, compassion, and knowledge of the illusory self he venerated. My poems are written in the spirit of Segalen's phrase "to conceive otherwise," which I believe to be the poet's essential task. My aim has been to explore, under the iconic signs of Segalen and Tibet, the armature of such conceits of the mind as identity and being and to conjure an imagined, timeless Tibet, a place not only of great and rugged beauty but of spiritual instruction and ethical hope.

DIÁNOIA (2016)

MAPPAH

A *mappah* is the embroidered ceremonial cloth laid over the open portion of the text between the scrolls of the Torah during those periods in the ceremony when it is not being read.

DIÁNOIA

This title is from the Greek. Number 1271 in *Strong's Concordance:*

> *diánoia* (from 1223 /*diá,* "thoroughly, from side-to-side," which intensifies 3539 /*noiéō,* "to use the mind," from 3563 /*noús,* "mind")—properly, movement from one side (of an issue) to the other to reach *balanced-*conclusions; full-orbed reasoning...that literally reaches "across to the other side" (of a matter).

NEW POEMS

COLLOQUIA

The quoted text in section I is from the work of the poet George Oppen (1908–1984). In section II, the quoted lines are from a *sadhana* written by the Tibetan Buddhist teacher Chögyam Trungpa Rinpoche (1939–1987). In section III, "LW" is Ludwig Wittgenstein (1889–1951). Portions of section IV are based on Dante's *Divine Comedy.*

OUR TIMES

This poem is part of *Tibet: A Sequence.* See note above for "Ode to the Sky on the Esplanade of the New."

Index of Titles and First Lines

Acknowledgments

I would like to thank the editors and publishers of my previous books of poetry for their support and encouragement: Coffee House Press, *In the Builded Place* (1989); Dos Madres Press, *A Look at the Door with the Hinges Off* (2006) and *Earth and Cave* (2006); Salt Publishers, *Exigent Futures: New and Selected Poems* (2003); Shearsman Books, *Beckmann Variations and Other Poems* (2010); Sumac Press, *Accidental Center* (1972); SUN, *Knowledge* (1979); Talisman House Publishers, *Wordflow: New and Selected Poems* (1997) and *Eschaton* (2009); Nightboat Books, *This Constellation Is a Name: Collected Poems 1965–2010* (2012) and *Dianoia* (2016). My thanks to the editors of the online journals *Jacket2* for publishing "Colloquia" and "Our Times" and *alligatorzine* for "The Whole Life" and "Re-Searches." I would also like to express my gratitude to the numerous editors of the many magazines, journals, anthologies, and online sites where these poems initially appeared. Deepest thanks to Edwin Frank, my editor at New York Review Books, for his guidance and counsel in preparing this volume, and to the publishing and production staff for making this book possible.

KINGSLEY AMIS COLLECTED POEMS: 1944–1979

GUILLAUME APOLLINAIRE ZONE: SELECTED POEMS
Translated by Ron Padgett

AUSTERITY MEASURES THE NEW GREEK POETRY
Edited by Karen Van Dyck

SZILÁRD BORBÉLY BERLIN-HAMLET
Translated by Ottilie Mulzet

NAJWAN DARWISH NOTHING MORE TO LOSE
Translated by Kareem James Abu-Zeid

W. S. GRAHAM *Selected by Michael Hofmann*

SAKUTARŌ HAGIWARA CAT TOWN
Translated by Hiroaki Sato

RYSZARD KRYNICKI OUR LIFE GROWS
Translated by Alissa Valles; Introduction by Adam Michnik

JOAN MURRAY DRAFTS, FRAGMENTS, AND POEMS:
THE COMPLETE POETRY
*Edited and with an introduction by Farnoosh Fathi; Preface by
John Ashbery*

EUGENE OSTASHEVSKY THE PIRATE WHO DOES NOT KNOW
THE VALUE OF PI
Art by Eugene and Anne Timerman

ELISE PARTRIDGE THE IF BORDERLANDS: COLLECTED POEMS

VASKO POPA *Selected and translated by Charles Simic*

J. H. PRYNNE THE WHITE STONES
Introduction by Peter Gizzi

WALT WHITMAN DRUM-TAPS: THE COMPLETE 1865 EDITION
Edited by Lawrence Kramer

ELIZABETH WILLIS ALIVE: NEW AND SELECTED POEMS